MW00900290

PSI

NATIONAL REAL ESTATE
LICENSE EXAM PREP

Pass Your Exam the First Time and without Stress!
10 Tips + 7 Practice Tests for Brokers and Salespeople
You Absolutely Must Know

BYRON BLAKE

Disclaimer

The content of this book has been checked and compiled with great care. For the completeness, correctness and topicality of the contents however no guarantee or guarantee can be taken over. The content of this book represents the personal experience and opinion of the author and is for entertainment purposes only. The content should not be confused with medical help.

There will be no legal responsibility or liability for damages resulting from counterproductive exercise or errors by the reader. No guarantee can be given for success. The author therefore assumes no responsibility for the non-achievement of the goals described in the book

4

TABLE OF CONTENTS

INTRODUCTION

PSI National Real Estate License Exam Preparation 2022 is an up-to-the-minute study guide created as a comprehensive resource for those writing the PSI National Real Estate License Exam. This eBook includes 7 practice tests that are just like the real thing, with explanations on every answer. It's a must have if you want to pass this test effortlessly.

So, you want to be a real estate agent, don't you? Welcome to the book that will help you through the process of becoming one. Many people find working as a real estate agent to be a highly enticing job option. This employment may be a good match for you if you enjoy looking at houses and other forms of real estate, as well as meeting and working with other people. When you combine having a flexible work schedule, practically owning your own firm, and being paid for your efforts and intellect, you have a career in real estate sales that is virtually ideal. The fact that real estate sales is a licensed profession, however, came to your notice somewhere along the line. Nevertheless, do not fret; I wrote this book expressly to aid you in earning your license. Are you ready to hear the complete story? Continue reading if you are going to become a real estate agent.

Real estate agents are needed to get a license in order to execute their trade in every state. Every state, at the very least, insists that you sit for and pass a state exam before you can receive that license. Some states demand more than merely an exam to be taken before applying. Following your choice to become a real estate salesperson or broker (brokers' licenses are generally gained after a length of time working as a salesperson), you must learn about the criteria for acquiring your license in your state of residence. As indicated in the title, this book is meant to aid you in preparing for and passing the state test. The book covers a vast variety of themes, including the principles of the profession, numerous real estate regulations, the nuances of owning and transferring property, and concerns such as contract law, leasing, and environmental standards, among many others. Do you believe that is a large sum of money? As a result, I cover everything you've ever wanted to know about numbers, from property appraisal to mortgage, tax, and investment calculations to financial planning advice. A state-administered examination is one of the phases required to become a licensed real estate agent.

While this may seem to be the most challenging step, be assured that this book will guide you through it. This chapter discusses ways for avoiding a total surprise throughout the testing process, as well as some details to keep an eye out for in your jurisdiction. Because real estate licenses are granted by individual states, the state in which you live is the ultimate authority on the state exam. The instructor of any needed relicensing course will almost certainly offer you with a copy of the state license law as well as any state-specific information you want on the exam. If you do not get information from your instructor, or if you reside in one of the few states that do not need relicensing, you may write to your state licensing agency or do an online search. While each state has its own agency responsible for real estate licensing, use a search engine such as Google may assist you in locating what you're searching for. Simply type your state's name into a search engine, followed by the terms "real estate license law," "real estate commission," "real estate board," or "real estate licensing agency." If you do not have access to a computer, you may call the information Centre in your state capital and request the phone number for the agency you are searching for, using any of the names I have provided above. Even if you search all of these names, you should contact your state's secretary of state or department of law through e-mail or telephone. It will almost probably point you in the right direction.

Chapter 1: Everything You Need to Know About your Exam

Every state requires real estate brokers and salespeople to be licensed. Specific requirements must be completed in order to be eligible for a license in each state, the District of Columbia, and the United States Virgin Islands. Additionally, licensure examinations and test designers are distinct. At the moment, there is no nationally standardized examination. Most states need a set number of classroom hours to become a salesperson or broker. You may determine what is required in your state by visiting the website of the real estate commission or board of real estate appraisal in your state or territory. In the same way, as there isn't a single and unique national real estate licensing exam for salespersons or brokers, there isn't a single and unique national test developer. State governments have several alternatives, including selecting their own test developer and requiring state-specific information to be tested alongside national content. When taking the test, the state-specific component will include questions on the state's real estate licensing legislation and the state's laws, rules, and directives regulating real estate inside the state's borders. The authority, function, and composition of your state's real estate commission or board are likely to be addressed on the exam. The format of the test, as well as how it is administered, varies per state. Salespeople and brokers often take the national component of the test, which has 80 questions, while the state segment contains between 40 and 60 questions, depending on the state. The test duration varies between two and four hours, depending on its length. A few test developers provide both paper-and-pencil and electronic versions of their examinations.

Certain other organizations provide just a computer-based exam. In some tests, replies are typed into computers using a standard keyboard, in others via a keypad, and in still others via touch screens. Candidates must go to a designated testing Center to take their exam.

After determining which test developer will administer the exam, Candidates can visit the test developer's website in order to find some information about the licensing exam they are going to attend. The website may include a handbook or other similar materials that will cover the exam in-depth.

Additionally, a content outline on your state's testing standards is given, which will be used for both the national component and the state-specific half of the exam. The strategy may contain the percentage of questions for each major topic. Consider the following things while doing your research: the location of the test, the frequency with which it will be conducted, the fee, how to register, and the kind of identification required to access the testing Center. If the choice is available, decide whether you wish to take the computer-based test or the paper-and-pencil version. Determine if you are authorized to use a calculator.

Using Successful Study and Test-Taking Techniques

This chapter will walk you through studying for the state real estate exam to pass it and make you become a real estate salesperson or broker fast and easily.

In the first half of the chapter, the reader can find some practical ways to prepare himself for the exam. In the second portion, it will be presented how to do the exam in the best way possible.

Rather than last-minute cramming, regular study seems to be the most successful technique for dealing with such subjects. In fact, it may happen that if you wait until the last minute to study and an emergency occurs (believe me, they always do), you will have no time to learn correctly. There is no need to study at a particular time of the day or for a specific amount of hours. You can study for a half-hour or an hour each night, followed by two or three hours on Saturday or Sunday. The goal is to dedicate regular time over a longer period to make the subject familiar to you. The tools you will need are this book, state-specific material, and the textbook for your relicensing course. While it may seem self-evident, it is something that every other teacher has warned you about, yet it is true. Take all necessary steps to study, including visiting the library if necessary. All real estate examinations, most notably the salesperson's examination, put a high priority on language.

You should pay particular attention to words written in italic in this book; you can highlight the term and its meaning; feel free to write whatever you want in this book. I aim to define a term in a single sentence so that you can focus on the definition. If you prefer to study by copying down information, you can create a list of terms and definitions or create three-by-five file cards for each phrase. Make a little note in the corner of each card describing the general subject to which the phrase refers. This will help you in the process of remembering the information in context. You may even expand on the card idea by creating flashcards. On one side of the card, write a sentence; on the reverse, write the definition. Then you may choose to have someone question you or do it by yourself.

Each state has its own set of real estate licensing laws, which often include more than just how to get a real estate license. It often involves certain business activities associated with the operation of a real estate agency. This material is often available in hard copy from the state's licensing agency or it can be downloaded from the state licensing agency's website (perform a web search for your state's site), or it can be delivered to you if you are required to finish a course before taking the exam. Along with reviewing the core topics in this book, make certain you become familiar with them and evaluate information particular to your state.

This information is included in the course that you are required to take.

For those of you who reside in jurisdictions where a course is not necessary, if the information is required for the exam, it will certainly be included in the booklet or in another exam preparation material provided by your state real estate licensing office. While preparing for the state exam, you must regularly evaluate your grasp of the subject. . It would be best to study still the chapters in which you excel to be safe, but if you don't have the opportunity, you'll know where to focus your limited time. After reading the material, analyzing your strong and weak points, and reviewing it again, it's time for a last run-through. If your scores continue to be wrong, review the subject and then retake the practice examinations on another day.

You must be able to determine the length (number of questions) and duration of the state exam. You may use this data to administer a self-paced practice exam that simulates the real one. To ensure that you will arrive safely, in good spirits, on time, and in the proper region, you must first identify the location and time of the exam and the estimated travel time. With such information in hand, you should acquire directions to the exam venue (no winging it) and learn if there will be large lineups to enter the exam or whether people are often turned away owing to test site congestion.

These features may vary across test venues, especially if your state administers the exam in many locations. You are now prepared to go. In this section, I'll discuss several test-taking tactics and ideas that will assist you in achieving the greatest potential score. Nothing can replace diligent work and preparation in the lead-up to the exam. And no strategy will assist you in passing if you aren't prepared enough. However, some of these tips might help you make the most of your study material while responding to the questions.

I'll let you in on a little test-taking secret: scan the exam quickly for what you know, but not so much that you will miss an answer that a more comprehensive read would have picked up on, and not so laboriously that you spend so much time studying the answers that you get them wrong or fail to finish the test. To begin, resolve a basic math problem. Subtract the total number of questions from the total time allocated to complete the exam. (You should be informed of this information before entering the testing facility.) Now it's time to establish some standards for yourself. Assume your exam will consist of 100 questions and will take two hours to finish. This allows you slightly more than a minute for each question.

You must have completed at least 50 questions before the end of the first hour. You must have completed 25 questions before the end of the first half-hour. You may move faster in certain sections and slower in others, but you must maintain a steady speed to ensure nothing is overlooked. As a teacher, nothing is more frustrating than having someone fail an exam because they could not finish it. Most students know the answers to at least a few of the eight or ten questions they haven't completed; they seldom get full credit for what they genuinely know. So, how are you going to pull yourself out of this pickle? Pass the exam quickly, question after question, replying only to those you are familiar with.

Rapid reading, but not rashly. Allow sufficient time for each question to allow you to grasp what it is asking and to go through all of the possible responses. If you are permitted to write in the exam book, jot down your replies. If you are required to instantly record your replies on the answer sheet, ensure that you always put the correct question number if you skip around. When you reach a question that you are unsure about, cross off the one or two solutions you know are wrong.

This will help you save some time in the future. If you're taking a computerized test, make sure to read the instructions carefully about question skipping. Once you've answered all of the questions, return to the ones you skipped. If you have difficulty with arithmetic, save the math puzzles until last. Always be careful of your time to avoid squandering it.

Chapter 2: Agent and Principal Relationships with Third Parties

Someone who has never taken the basic real estate course may suppose that the title of this chapter refers to the laws regulating the operation of a real estate agency; nevertheless, this is only partially true. However, as everyone who has taken that introductory course knows, the phrase "law of agency" refers to the corpus of law that controls the relationship between a buyer or seller and their real estate broker or agent. Regulations control the establishment and operation of a real estate agency. It establishes the legal basis for the aforementioned link.

While preparing for the exam, there are a few key terms to remember. In legal terminology, an agent is someone who has been given the power or capability to act on behalf of another, with the "other" being the principal who has authorized the agent to act on their behalf.

Real estate agents represent both buyers and sellers of property, depending on the transaction. The principal is represented in the transaction by either a licensed salesperson employed by a real estate broker or by the broker acting as an agent on the principal's behalf. A real estate broker is the licensed owner-manager of a real estate firm who recruits agents (also known as sales associates) to work for the company. An individual must get a state license and be hired by a real estate broker to practice real estate. In comparison to agents, brokers often have more years of experience selling real estate and have taken more advanced real estate courses. All listings that come into a real estate brokerage are under the broker's name, not the seller's agent. Consider the following scenario involving a typical real estate transaction.

As the agent and principal, you are assisting a client who wants to sell their townhouse and the buyer, referred to in this context as the third party, or customer, and their agent from another real estate agency. Employer, real estate broker, and broker representing the other agent are all loitering in the background, keeping an eye on you. The principal assigned power to the agent to do a certain duty, such as selling real estate, on the principal's behalf. The principal and the agent (broker) enter into a contract that details exactly what that one thing is.

Additionally, the agreement will describe how the assignment will be accomplished, such as by creating several listings for the property, as well as the commission that the agent will earn if the work is completed correctly. In general, a contract between a principal and an agent (broker) empowers the agent (broker) to do several activities on behalf of the principal, such as exhibiting a property to potential tenants, verifying renters' references, and negotiating the lease.

Buyer's & Agency Representative

The principal, who is the buyer in this case, and the real estate agent who represents the client, have established a buyer agency relationship. The real estate agent looks out for the buyer's best interests throughout the transaction. This occurs when the buyer and seller are represented by the same agent from the same company in the same real estate transaction (also known as dual agency).

Representative agency: Dual representation has the disadvantage of the agent being unable to represent either side due to potential conflicts of interest appropriately. To address this problem, the designated agency was founded. When a broker hires another real estate agent in the same office to represent a buyer or seller, that agent must be located in the same office as the broker. Generally, the purchaser bears the cost.

The Relationship Between Agency and Client

A principal may contact a real estate brokerage for several reasons. The principal may seek to acquire or dispose of real estate. The principal may want to rent rather than sell their property in rare instances. Additionally, a principal might be a developer looking to acquire many parcels of property or an investor wishing to acquire land, homes, or other structures. The agent-principal relationship is governed by state real estate licensing laws, rules, and regulations in all circumstances.

Types of Listing Agreements

The listing contract (or listing agreement) is stipulated between the seller and the broker (the agent's supervisor), not between the agent and the seller. There are several forms of listing agreements, and unless otherwise mentioned, they are virtually always in writing.

The listing contract details what the principal authorizes the agent to perform, such as selling or leasing real estate for a certain price in exchange for a specified fee over a specified period. Both the property owners and the agent representing them must sign the contract (broker).

There are four common kinds of listing agreements: In the real estate sector, terminology such as (1) exclusive right to sell, (2) exclusive agency, (3) open listing, and (4) net listing is often employed. The least common kind of listing is on the internet, whereas the most common type is exclusive right to sell. Each listing type safeguards the broker's compensation.

Exclusive right to sell

The exclusive right to sell listings allows the broker to market a certain piece of property exclusively. It is the most advantageous listing for both the broker and the principal since the broker is confident that they will be reimbursed if the property sells. It incentivizes the broker to make every attempt to locate a buyer who is ready, willing, and capable of purchasing the property.

While the principal is always free to sell their property, if the principal or someone other than the broker sells the property—for example, the principal's son—the broker retains the fee. Suppose another broker locates a buyer who is willing and able to acquire the property and the principal agrees. In that case, the original broker will normally split the commission with the second broker. Exceptions may be made. If the situation is reversed, the original broker wants the same treatment.

Exclusive agency listing

Due to the exclusive agency listing, the broker has the only right to promote the property. In contrast, the broker is not compensated if the principal sells the property. The principal may not transfer the listing to another broker while the contract with the original broker is still in place.

Open Listing

An open listing, also known as a general listing or a nonexclusive listing, enables the seller to market the property simultaneously to many brokers. Since the probability of locating a ready, willing, and able buyer is distributed across several brokers, there is no certainty that a broker will earn a commission. Additionally, the principal may maintain the right to sell the property on their own if the case warrants it. If this occurs, no broker will be compensated for the transaction. This listing type is more prevalent in commercial real estate than in residential real estate.

Net listing

This kind of listing may be forbidden or limited in your region, so verify your state's real estate rules before proceeding. A net listing is one in which the broker receives the difference (the net) between the selling and asking prices. For instance, if the net price is $1 million (what the owner is willing to accept) and you sell the house for $1.1 million, you keep $100,000 as a commission on the transaction. If the house sells for $990,000, on the other hand, you will not get a commission. Depending on the conditions, internet listings may be exclusive or nonexclusive.

Multiple Listing

Multiple listings are not synonymous with the four listings mentioned above. Multiple listing systems (MLS) or multiple listing services (MLS) are advertising methods for real estate. Brokers may share listings—and commissions—via a multiple listing service (MLS). When a broker in a multiple listing service (MLS) enters into a listing agreement with a principal, the broker submits the listing to the MLS clearinghouse, which publishes it for all MLS members to see. Consequently, a growing number of brokers are actively seeking a buyer who is prepared, willing, and capable of purchasing the principal's house. The listing broker receives the commission, which is often split 50/50 with the selling broker, who brings the buyer to the table.

Chapter 3: Everything You Need to Know About Agency Law

According to your prior experience, a Hollywood agent is probably the kind of agent you are most familiar with. As a consequence, let's examine the meaning of the word "agent." An agent's work description includes many activities that have to be done before and after major events and film premieres. The fact that an agent represents a client suggests that the agent will always work in the client's best interest while negotiating deals on the client's behalf. The agent will make every effort to get the best possible position for the client at the lowest possible cost, or they will make every effort to secure the client a bigger dressing room at the production studio.

When it comes to real estate agents, there are no exceptions. They serve as advocates for their clients and always operate in the best interests of their clients. Only this time, the goal is not to have more lovely bodies or more dressing room space. The majority of the time, the motives are to get a higher price for a house or to sell it more quickly. Whether they operate out of Hollywood or Topeka, the link between agents and the clients they represent as fraught with expectations, all of which are satisfied by the agents.

This chapter will include An examination of the critical agency relationship and its essential players and also how to establish such a connection and detail the many characteristics of relationships between agents, principals (also known as clients), and customers. The reader will be informed about payday (who pays an agent and when) and how to end an agency arrangement. You should study each chapter in this book since they all offer material that will assist you in answering questions on the real estate exam you will be taking. However, it is critical that you pay particular attention to the content included in this chapter.

Real estate agents continue to be misunderstood by individuals who buy and sell houses and other forms of property. Despite the improvement in the situation, several states are active in ensuring that their real estate agents understand the agency connection, act correctly and effectively, and explain the relationship's intricacies to the individuals who utilize their services.

Although the precise types of agency relationships and the regulations governing agencies differ significantly by state, the information I present in this chapter is highly generic and hence applicable in most (if not all) states. Consequently, you must pay close attention to how your state addresses the problem of agency so that you are completely informed about agency rules and how agency contacts are conducted in your jurisdiction. States have increased the number of hours required for agency law training in recent years, which has resulted in a higher emphasis on this subject on state licensing tests.

Preparation is critical if you want to pass your state's exam without being caught up by agency law questions. This website section contains information on some of the essential parts of agency law, whom you represent, and how the agency connection between you and your client is formed. Who you are and what you represent may seem to be a straightforward question, but is this the case? Many real estate agents, buyers, and sellers are either unaware of what constitutes an agency relationship or seem to have forgotten about it along the way.

Simultaneously with providing you information about who you represent in a real estate transaction, it will be explained why this scenario is questionable. Each agency relationship includes several participants, and it is important to understand your position in the partnership. An agent is someone who has been authorized to engage in a legal case on behalf of another person's interests. Three types of agents are given in ascending order of authority: Specialization is required in some professional aspects. For example, in a single transaction, an agent is someone who has been hired by another party to represent them. A special agent, in general, is a real estate agent who represents a buyer or seller in the purchase or sale of a residence. In certain jurisdictions, these agents are referred to as specific agents. General agents are those who operate on behalf of an individual over a wide range of activities or across a collection of connected activities. A general agent or property manager is a term that refers to an agent that handles many functions, such as collecting rent, paying bills, approving repairs and negotiating leases.

Consequently, you should guarantee that you can speak fluently in the state's official language. The universal agent is often referred to as a general agent (see the next bullet point). The universal agent is an agent who represents a client in all matters and conditions, someone who has been empowered to act on behalf of another party in all real estate transactions.

Simply put, the primary (client) is the one with whom you have an agency relationship, that is, the individual who has allowed you to represent them. Third parties include customers, i.e., those whom you do not represent. And this lineup applies whether you are representing a buyer or a seller in a transaction. While "warning" may be a harsh term here, the fact that this is the point in the explanation many people get perplexed is critical.

However, it's critical to note that the uncertainty exists primarily due to the way the real estate industry has functioned for the last 10,000 years. (So it wasn't 10,000 years ago, but at some time during the Stone Age, a real estate agent may have attempted to pitch someone on a wonderful cool tropical cave with an ocean view.) Because real estate brokerage has developed into a profession, it is not uncommon for real estate brokers to represent sellers while spending the bulk of their time representing buyers. Most people who have bought or sold a property and dealt with an agent will understand exactly what I'm talking about. When a real estate broker signs an agreement to act as an agent to sell someone's house, the agent undertakes not to contact the seller again except to bring possible purchasers to the property.

Meanwhile, Mr. and Mrs. Buyer are chauffeured about looking for houses on Saturdays by the agency. Mr. and Mrs. Buy are the customers. This arrangement is totally OK; the agent, who spends so much time with them, is so polite and helpful, and may even be an excellent match for their single relative, is really representing the seller. On the other side, buyers develop the belief that the agent is working for them. Additionally, the agent begins to act in the same way that he does.

The term "buyer agency" was coined to clarify matters, particularly for buyers, for when an agent represents a buyer rather than a seller. In this case, the buyer is the primary or client, while the seller is the customer. The incidence and legitimacy of buyer agency regulations vary by state; therefore before participating in any transactions, you should study any buyer agency limits specifically enforced in your state. Dual agency is a term that refers to a scenario in which the same real estate agent represents both parties to a transaction, most often a buyer and a seller. While dual agency may be prohibited in your area, it is permitted in a huge number of other jurisdictions, so this book will provide some material that should be enough to Pass any exam questions on the issue.

To determine if dual agency is lawful in your state, you must first review the state's legislation, and then determine under what conditions it is permissible. Consider the following examples: you agree to act as a buyer's agent on Mr. and Mrs. Buyer's behalf to assist them in their home hunt. You get a phone call from Mr. and Mrs. Seller, who have been trying unsuccessfully to sell their home for months, motivating you to accept their offer to act as their agent.

The Buyers agree to make an offer after visiting Mr. and Mrs. Seller's home, which you will arrange for them to undertake as part of your agreement with them.

The parties to this transaction have retained your services, and you are acting on their behalf. There is a duality of agency in this situation. To make this lawful, if your state permits it, the most common method is to notify both Buyers and Sellers of your dual agency status and get their consent to continue serving both parties.

The informed consent procedure is the name given to the process of getting informed consent. For instance, in some jurisdictions, such as California, the notion that a broker is only an intermediary in a transaction between two parties is gaining traction. Numerous countries have permitted a kind of transactional brokerage, which permits a broker to operate as a middleman between buyers and sellers while still getting compensated for his or her services. The broker connects the buyer and seller, negotiates the transaction's conditions, and handles some or all of the accompanying paperwork. However, a critical difference is that the transactional broker does not represent either side in the transaction. For additional information, you should consult your state's real estate laws to determine whether this type of arrangement exists and, if so, what the new arrangement is called in your state, what brokers are called in this situation (as they may no longer be considered agents), and what the fundamental duties and responsibilities are for brokers in this situation (as they are no longer considered fiduciaries).

Agent-principal agreements

Express agency is a type of agency relationship in which the agent and principal express their desire to enter into an agency relationship and the agent agrees to act as the principal's agent by signing a document stating their desire to enter into an agency relationship and the agent's agreement to represent the principal. Orally or in writing, the parties communicate or convey their intentions via words. The legal enforceability of an oral agreement establishing an agency relationship varies by state, so be careful to check your local laws. The most often used kind of written agreement is a listing agreement or a buyer's agency agreement, which are explored in further depth in the following two sections. It is possible to establish an agency relationship between two persons based on their behavior, which is referred to as inferred agency. Even though no legal agreement has been reached or documented, the agent and principal operate as though they are in a formal agency relationship. While it is conceivable that the two parties did not intend to create an implicit agency relationship, one may nevertheless be formed.

If you're having difficulty comprehending these terms, consider what occurred to Ms. Seller. Ms. Seller is selling her home independently, and she has posted a "for sale" sign in her yard to garner interest. You pass by, see the sign, and choose to enter. You identify yourself as a real estate professional and inquire about the property. She notifies you that she is not interested in listing the property with a real estate agent or agency. She does inform you that you are welcome to bring any prospective buyers who want to see the house. You bring Mr. and Mrs. Buyer the next day, who have fallen in love with the place and are ready to make an offer. You notify Ms. Seller of your plans and start the selling negotiation process. When it comes to commissions and lawsuits, only a court of law can determine definitively, but you and Ms. Seller have very likely developed an implicit agency relationship due to both of your actions in this case.

Agency by implication: When a principal does not restrict an agent from going above and beyond the agent's customary responsibilities, the illusion of an agency relationship between the parties is created. If you are the property owner, you may ask your agent to conduct a tour of the premises for a potential tenant.... Despite the fact that you did not authorize the agent to negotiate a lease directly, the agency proceeded with the discussions. Because the tenant believes the agent has authority, an agency by estoppel has been formed. In the instance of an agency constituted by ratification, the agency is created by recognizing the circumstances that resulted in its formation post facto.

Consider the following scenario: a real estate agent negotiates a contract for a house that the seller is selling for without the seller's approval or interaction. One day, the agent appears with a completed contract in hand, ready for the seller to sign and accept the transaction's conditions as written. When the seller accepted the contract, an agency by ratification was very certainly created, since the seller approved the agent's actions. It is a "probably" because the agent wants to be compensated for his services and may have to sue the seller to get payment. In this instance, the courts determine whether an agency relationship existed from the beginning of the conversations by examining whether the seller accepted or verified the agent's activities by accepting the deal.

The marriage of agency and self-interest: The term "agents having a financial interest in the property" refers to agents who have some financial stake in the property they are selling. Take the example of a part-time trader who is also an architect. After agreeing to design numerous homes for a builder, who would then furnish the broker/architect with listings for finished houses for sale, both parties proceed with their plans. In essence, since the broker/architect has invested in the project, the builder cannot cancel the agency agreement with them. Bear in mind that the broker/architect is not tying one activity to another, which would constitute an antitrust violation. A tie-in agreement would have been made if the broker had said that for him to sell the finished homes, the builder would also have to hire him (pay him) to design the homes. When an agency and an interest are combined, it's as if the broker/architect is investing their own money in the project. Often, a formal agreement is utilized to establish agency relationships between buyers and sellers. Buyer agency agreements are between buyers and sellers, while listing agreements are between sellers and buyers. (How did you arrive at your conclusion?) Numerous agreements come under each of the two groups. Many of the aspects contained in various types of agreements are the same in terms of the duties that must be completed.

The contrasts mostly pertain to the circumstances in which an agent will be reimbursed for their services or will not be compensated at all. The issue of broker fee payment, which is covered in further detail later in this chapter in the section "Making Money (No, not at the Copy Machine)," is sometimes tied to who is the procuring cause of the buyer or seller in the transaction. To qualify as a procuring cause, an individual must first seek a buyer or seller and then complete the transaction. It is often referred to as the crucial person in bringing a buyer and a seller together. Additionally, it might be defined as the broker who brought a ready, willing, and able buyer into the deal at a price acceptable to all sides.

Selling a property with the right of first refusal: A broker is awarded exclusive marketing rights to advertise the property on behalf of the seller under this kind of listing agreement. The broker is reimbursed regardless of whether the property is sold, which is a critical point to notice since it distinguishes this form of listing agreement from others. To be more precise: Even if the owner sells the property without the aid of a real estate agent while the listing agreement is in effect, the owner is still obligated to pay the broker the agreed-upon fee.

Exclusive agency listing: A broker is hired to act as the owner's exclusive agent, representing them in all elements of the property's marketing and advertising. Naturally, the broker will earn a commission if the property is sold. However, if the property is sold without the help of a broker, the property owner is not obligated to pay the broker's fee.

Explicit listing: Have you noticed anything that was omitted from the title of this kind of listing? The term "exclusive" has been deleted from the contract, since the property owner has the right to engage as many agents as required to sell the property. No broker is authorized to act only on behalf of the property owner in a transaction. In certain quarters, this kind of listing is referred to as a nonexclusive or generic listing. The owner of a property that is freely marketed but receives no help from a broker is under no obligation to pay a broker commission.

The following is a list of net addresses: When a net listing is formed, a broker is hired to sell the property for a certain sum of money, referred to as the net amount or net price, as decided by the seller. The broker retains any amount above the net price. As a result, if you accept a net listing on a property for which the owner anticipates a $200,000 profit on the sale but the home ultimately sells for $225,000, you get a commission of $25,000 on the transaction. Please bear in mind that many states restrict online listings while others encourage them. Certain countries authorize it only if the seller is told in writing of the agent's maximum commission that may be earned during the first listing agreement. Consult your state's regulations about this kind of listing to see whether it is legal. Frequently, inquiries about online listings are made.

Even though I discuss fiduciary responsibilities to ensure that you have a good general understanding of the subject for exam purposes, you should still research your local state's interpretation of fiduciary duties to ensure that your answers are more consistent with specific questions on the state exam. Because fiduciary obligations are the bedrock of the agency relationship, the test writers want to verify that you understand your obligations as a representative. Prepare to answer any questions on this topic at the state exams. As a real estate agent, you often deal with large sums of money. The word "binder" or "earnest money" is most often used to refer to this money. These funds are placed into the buyer's account and count toward the buyer's down payment. They ultimately become the seller's property; however, the broker may hold them for a long time. You may write a check to the broker. Apart from the money received from the buyer or the sale, the broker may be entrusted with additional funds.

Your fiduciary duties include the duty to account for any funds entrusted to your care. The majority of states mandate that client and customer money be stored in a separate bank account from the broker's business account to avoid client and customer funds from being mixed or merged with the broker's business or personal finances. Commingling is illegal. Conversion, or the act of using client or customer funds for the agent's personal or business expenses, is also forbidden. Care, as a wide and encompassing concept, is best characterized as agents exerting their best efforts and abilities most effectively on behalf of their client's specific interests.

The client's activity expectations under the care component of fiduciary obligations include aiding a selling client in identifying a realistic asking price for a property and then advertising the property aggressively. When a buyer is the client, encouraging them to hire a house inspection and providing information on similar property prices are regular components of the care offering. The agent is expected to maintain the strictest confidentiality regarding all information that may jeopardize the client's interests and any personal information the client requests to be kept confidential, even if the agent believes that making the information public will not harm the client.

The desperate need to sell a house that a selling customer has as a result of a financial situation must always be concealed. To ensure secrecy, a buyer client's equally urgent desire to find a house before the school year starts and the buyer client's ability to pay more for a property than they are now offering must be kept hidden. Client information that may promote the customer's interests over the client's interests must be kept absolutely confidential. Depending on your jurisdiction, confidentiality requirements may be considered a component of the fiduciary responsibility of loyalty. Under the provisions of your fiduciary duty of disclosure, it is your job as an agent to disclose any facts known to you that are advantageous to your client.

Disclosure refers to information that may be beneficial to the client even if the customer has not requested it. While you, as an agent, may be aware that the town is having a tax reassessment that has the potential to drastically modify the taxes on all of the town's residences, your buyer client is acquiring a property for the first time and has no concept what a reassessment is or how it would affect them. If you haven't previously, you should be able to respond to state exam questions about reassessment After studying Chapter 16 of this book.

Regardless of whether or not your clients were aware of the impending reassessment, you are expected to tell them of the impending reassessment as a buyer's agent. Additionally, disclosure applies to information that may be harmful to your client's interests and that your client has asked you to keep confidential.

Perhaps your purchaser informs you that they have just encountered financial issues that make acquiring a mortgage difficult. Whether or not your buyer client wishes confidentiality, you must tell your seller customer that the buyer may have difficulty getting a mortgage to acquire the house in issue. If you wish to understand more about an agent's duties to a client, continue reading this chapter to the section "Meeting Obligations: The Relationship Between an Agent and a Customer."

The word "disclosure" has a broad definition. For instance, the agent's responsibility to present all offers to the selling client in a timely way is considered to be part of disclosure. The agent's decision to acquire his principal's property must be disclosed. Self-dealing occurs when an agent acquires a house that he has listed for sale. Additional parties to the transaction, such as a family member of the listing agent who is interested in acquiring the house, must be disclosed. If the information has the potential to assist your client in any way, or if it has the potential to do him harm if he is unaware, it must be shared with him. Maintain an awareness of how the disclosure needed of agents as part of their fiduciary obligation varies from the disclosure required of sellers, who are expected to disclose latent and serious concerns.

When a seller (whether or not she or he employs the services of a real estate agent) becomes aware of a problem with a property that is not readily apparent during a standard inspection (rather than during a special professionally performed home inspection) and/or that would have a material effect on the buyer's decision to purchase the property, they are required to inform the buyer in many states. Bear in mind that this kind of disclosure is exempt from the fiduciary responsibility of secrecy (mentioned before) and the requirement of obedience. For further information, check the part later in this chapter titled "Discovering Defects."

A significant reason states establish agency disclosure requirements, which require agents to inform everyone involved exactly who they represent and what that entails, is the federal government-imposed fiduciary responsibility of disclosure to the principal. Too often, buyer customers get so comfortable with their real estate agent that they provide information that might be damaging to them during the bargaining phase of a real estate purchase. The customer either forgets or never completely comprehends that the agent is operating on behalf of the seller in terms of fiduciary duties and obligations. Loyalty entails consistently putting your client's interests ahead of everyone else's, even your own. You may need to reread the last sentence – including your own.

You will never benefit by acting in your client's best interest, and vice versa.

Consider the following hypothetical situation: You represent a purchaser who desires to bid $200,000 on a property. You know how much the seller is willing to take ($180,000), and you're compensated as a percentage of the home's eventual sale price. In other words, the more money you make as an agent, the higher the home's price, correct? I'm going to be direct: Even though disclosing the seller's acceptable price is counter to your interests and will result in you earning less money, you are compelled to notify the buyer since it is the appropriate and legally necessary thing to do. You must inform your buying consumer that the lowest offer should be made.

Unless and until this rule is followed, you will be in violation of your fiduciary responsibility of loyalty and will profit at the expense of your client. As an agent, you owe it to your principal to follow his or her instructions, which is referred to as obedience. Obedience is often referred to as "faithful performance" in some publications. The only exception to the duty of compliance is if the client's instructions are illegal or immoral, in which case the duty of obedience does not apply. If a selling client provides you with marketing instructions that violate a provision of fair housing laws, your fiduciary duty of compliance does not require you to violate the law to comply with the client's request.

Buyer Agency Agreements

A buyer agency agreement requires the broker to always operate in the buyer's best interest throughout the transaction. In other words, the broker may counsel the customer on issues such as the best property to meet the buyer's specifications and the best price to pay for the property. If a broker is involved in a dual agency, they cannot advise a buyer if the property the broker is representing is too costly or if another property meets the client's needs better.

Buyer agency agreements may be classified into three basic types: exclusive buyer agency, exclusive agency buyer agency, and open buyer agency. The most typical sort of buyer agency arrangement is an exclusive buyer agency agreement. For the most part, a buyer agency agreement has the same characteristics as a listing agreement, such as a time period and cost. These are terminated in the same manner as listing agreements. As specified in the buyer's agreement, the fee is often taken from the seller's compensation to their broker. The agreement also covers contingencies such as a listing contract that does not permit commission sharing. Following that, the buyer will be forced to pay the seller the buyer agency agreement fee. In all jurisdictions, buyer agency agreements must be in writing to be legally enforceable.

Exclusive Buyer agency agreement

The exclusive buyer agency agreement, sometimes referred to as the exclusive right to represent, vests the broker with the only authority to help a buyer in locating a property to purchase. Even if the buyer acquires a house without the aid of the broker throughout the length of the agreement, the broker must be reimbursed for their services.

Termination of Agency/Agreements

When it comes to real estate agents and brokers, their biggest desire is that the agency would conclude with a pleased buyer and seller at the closing, a process known as termination by performance. This is not always the case, though. States recognize a variety of distinct procedures for terminating agencies or agreements. Conduct thorough study about what is permissible in your state. Disagreements between the principal and the agent or broker, as well as legal issues, are common causes for termination.

The former consists of the following: When the listing contract's time limit has elapsed and no buyer has been identified, the principal and agent reach an agreement. Resignation of the agent, also known as renunciation by the agent; termination of the agent by the principal, also known as revocation by the principal. ages from a resigned agent, and an agent may be able to seek damages from a dismissed principal, depending on the circumstances.

The following statutes regulate the termination of agency ties as a result of the following events: All of these scenarios are possible: property destruction; government seizure of the property through eminent domain; bankruptcy of either the principal or the agent; death of either the principal or the agent; and declaration of incompetence of either the principal or the agent.

Chapter 4: Interests, Estates, and ownership

Improvements made by an owner are often viewed as permanent and, consequently, as transferable real property. Renter modifications are often seen as transitory, and the tenant is responsible for removing them before leaving the premises. This is particularly true for commercial tenants who may choose to modify a property to meet their unique business requirements. Although it is infrequent for company leases to say that all fixtures and fittings become the landlord's property, many commercial leases do not demand that all fixtures and fittings be restored to their original condition unless expressly specified. As you may imagine, the specifics of these restrictions are rigorously addressed before signing. If there is any doubt about whether an item is a chattel or real estate, the item is often specified in the contract to minimize misunderstanding. A principal may specify in the listing contract that they will remove the chandelier from the dining room and not include it in the sale of the house. If the buyer begs the seller to leave it as a condition of the sale and the seller agrees, the agreement should be included as an attachment to the final sales contract.

When a person acquires real estate, they may acquire a variety of ownership rights as part of the transaction. When a property is acquired, all surface, subsurface, mineral rights, and water and air rights are instantly transferred with the title. The exceptions include condominium and cooperative ownership. Continue reading a few sections ahead to learn more about Owning in Common. These rights may be incorporated in the ownership structure of a condominium unless the developer has already sold them to another buyer. If these rights have not been sold, they are deemed part of the common area, and the condo purchaser will own just a percentage of the common area upon acquiring the unit.Additionally, it is likely that the developer did not acquire these rights from the original owner. They may have been purposely left out of the developer's purchase. If these rights were conveyed together with the property when the co-op was created, the business becomes the owner.

In this case, the co-op purchaser would retain a part of these rights as a result of their ownership of the business's shares.

The owner of a property owns the air space above it. On the other hand, federal aviation rules and local zoning regulations limit this right. When a property owner executes an easement, it often extends to all of the property owner's heirs and assigns. The easement may be included in a deed or a written easement, and if it is meant to remain when ownership changes, it is referred to as "running with the land." Air rights are often used when a property owner desires to profitably sell the air rights above their land to another party, typically a developer.

Local zoning restrictions govern the additional development's height. The original property owner maintains title to both the land and the original structure, while the developer retains just ownership of the additional shops built to the structure. An owner may sell air rights in exchange for constructing a pedestrian bridge over their property to connect two buildings on the same plot of land. The term "bundle of rights" refers to the collection of property rights that property owners possess. They are the rights to live, use, and enjoy one's property in its whole, which may include land, water, air, and other natural resources. Additionally, the bundle of rights includes the right to profitably utilize the property, such as farming or leasing, as well as the right to sell, bequeath, give, or lease the property in whole or in part, as well as the ability to transfer ownership of the land. Additionally, the bundle of rights suggests that the owner has entire authority over all of these rights and is free to do nothing with them if desired. However, not all estates have the whole range of ownership rights that are often associated with them. Property may be acquired in a variety of ways. Individuals, married couples, couples cohabiting, trusts, corporations, and other legal organizations may acquire, possess, and sell real estate. Additionally, there are specific property ownership structures, such as condominiums. Tenancy in common is the most often used form of joint color ownership, despite the fact that it does not provide tenants with a right of succession. This is the kind of ownership that two unmarried adults would almost certainly enter if they want to acquire a home together. Tenancy in common vests each person with an undivided interest in the property; nevertheless, the degree of ownership varies according to the circumstances. It is not required to split the funds evenly. Additionally, each tenant has severalty ownership, which means that each tenant is free to dispose of their interest in the property as they please without seeking agreement from the other tenants. To safeguard his investment, a tenant may refinance it, sell it, or leave it to a third party in his will. When considering the property ownership of married spouses, there are two distinct ownership forms: tenancy by the whole and common property. On the other side, community property ownership is not recognized by all, or even the majority, of governments. Apart from that, not all jurisdictions recognize tenancy by the whole of the property.

Tenancy by the entirety

Property is owned jointly by the two partners in marriage as if they were one entity. They both have the right to survive the death of the other in addition to possessing undivided and equal ownership of the property. Neither spouse may sell, give away, will, or mortgage the property in issue without the other spouse's consent. When a marriage is dissolved by divorce, the tenancy by the entirety is replaced by a tenancy in common. The four unities, as well as the individual unity, must be met before the whole group is awarded tenancy. Property obtained during a marriage is considered jointly and equally owned by both spouses, while community property regimes do not recognize a right of survivorship if a couple acquires property during their marriage. A spouse may leave a portion of his or her inheritance to the surviving spouse, to a child, or to whoever the person wishes to benefit from the estate. In California, property that a spouse held before the marriage or acquired during the marriage is not considered community property. Independent property is what it is, and the original owner or inheriting owner has full authority over how the thing is utilized and disposed of.

Along with the four basic types of property ownership described above, four additional types of property ownership do not fit neatly into the categories just discussed: ownership of condominiums, cooperatives, planned unit developments (planned housing developments such as townhouse complexes), and timeshares, the newest wrinkle in the world of property ownership. Purchasing a condominium unit entails the exchange of a deed between two individuals or couples. The purchaser receives ownership of a specific unit as well as common areas such as the lobby and fitness Centre, as well as the ground under and surrounding the building. Condo owners are expected to pay a monthly fee known as a maintenance fee to cover the costs of administration and upkeep of the condominium. A volunteer board of directors oversees the building's functioning, defines policy, and establishes rules and regulations for condominium members. Condominium owners are liable for real estate taxes on both their individual units and fractional interests in shared amenities.

Cooperative apartment ownership

A cooperative apartment is acquired via the purchase of shares in the underlying organization. Consequently, the purchaser does not get ownership of a particular unit but rather a proprietary lease on that unit. Similar to a condominium, a cooperative has a board of directors, a monthly fee, and a management company that is responsible for the building's care. In contrast to a condominium, a cooperative's monthly fee covers both maintenance and property taxes. To become a cooperative member, you must pass an interview with the board of directors and a review of financial documents. PUDs (planned unit developments) are ongoing undertakings. A townhouse might be a condominium or a planned unit development (PUD), which is defined as a collection of residential, commercial, and industrial buildings created and completed by a single developer. Additionally, a PUD may contain single-family houses, or it may be entirely composed of residential buildings. In a planned unit development (PUD), the property owner controls the ground under and around their unit. The PUD is not a co-owner of the land. The common areas of a PUD, such as parking lots and recreation areas, are owned by all unit owners. Residents elect a board of directors, also referred to as a homeowner's association (HOA), to oversee the management company that maintains the PUD, to develop policy, and to draught PUD rules, among other things. Property owners are personally liable for their taxes.

Timeshares

A timeshare gives a person a fractional ownership stake in a property in return for the opportunity to use the property for a certain period of time, often one or two weeks each year. The property in question is often an apartment in a vacation area or a hotel room in the city's center. A timeshare is an interest in real estate that the timeshare owner owns in fee simple. You will be charged an annual maintenance fee when you purchase a timeshare. Any form of corporate organization may own real estate, from the biggest Fortune 500 firm with sprawling office campuses to a small pet adoption charity that acquires the building that houses its shelter to a group of two friends purchasing a property to rent out. If you choose to work in commercial real estate as a real estate agent, you are more likely to deal with commercial property ownership.

Partnerships

Partnerships are classified into two types: general partnerships and limited partnerships. A growing number of jurisdictions have passed uniform partnership or uniform limited liability partnership laws to regulate the functioning of partnerships investing in real estate. General partnerships include agreement on all elements of a property's functioning, including its sale or mortgage, as well as its management. Additionally, all partners are jointly and severally accountable for the partnership's operations, and partners are taxed in proportion to the amount of their interest or investment in the partnership. When you create a limited liability partnership, each partner's liability is limited to the value of their contribution to the partnership. Typically, one partner is in control of the partnership's day-to-day activities. Corporations may acquire real estate for various reasons, including investment, the construction of their own facilities, or the development and sale of their own property. Although a corporation may have thousands of investors and thousands of employees, it is treated as an individual entity under the law and hence enjoys exclusive ownership (tenancy in severalty) of its property. It is typical for a corporation's responsibility to be limited to the amount invested by its shareholders, and this is also true for me.

Chapter 5: The Purpose of Fair Housing Laws

You may describe the fair housing laws of the United States as well as the laws of each state and each city in a single sentence: you are not allowed to discriminate in the sale or leasing of real estate. Regardless of whether the property is being sold or leased, the pronoun "you" applies to both you, the realtor, and you, the property owner who is referred to as the "you." The goal of fair housing legislation is to provide a level playing field for all persons when it comes to the choosing of a place to live. Fair housing laws are in place to accomplish this goal. One of the most important factors to consider is the financial status and housing wish list of potential purchasers or renters, not the seller's or landlord's anti-immigrant sentiments towards these individuals. The enforcement of fair housing standards serves as a substantial public restraint on the rights of private property owners while these regulations are in place.

Additionally, the federal Department of Housing and Urban Development has made it a top priority to guarantee that fair housing standards are implemented by both landlords and tenants. According to the Fair Housing Act, people with disabilities who rent property are authorized to make "reasonable modifications" to the property to be able to live there. When the tenant's lease ends and they vacate the premises, the property must be restored to the state it was in prior to the modification being performed. It is negotiable under the conditions that the adjustment "would not interfere with the... [future] use and enjoyment" of the property.

The Americans with Disabilities Act (ADA) was enacted by Congress in 1992 to protect people with disabilities from being discriminated against in the workplace and other settings. While the Fair Housing Act outlaw's discrimination in housing, the Americans with Disabilities Act (ADA) prohibits discrimination in a broad variety of contexts, including the workplace. In terms of real estate, the Americans with Disabilities Act (ADA) protects the right of individuals with disabilities to enter public spaces while also requiring the elimination of architectural barriers in new building projects. Title III of the Americans with Disabilities Act incorporates the Americans with Disabilities Act Accessibility Guidelines, which deal with the identification and removal of architectural impediments in both existing and new construction. Whenever a barrier cannot be removed from a historical construction, it is necessary to investigate other solutions. In order to avoid participating in illegal activities, you should be aware of the words "blockbusting," "steering," and "redlining," among other terms.

According to the list of illegal crimes, blockbusting is the practice of persuading property owners to sell or rent their property by preying on their fears and with the intent of making a profit from the transaction. It is not enough for Joe Smith to be convinced to sell his house and move by a realtor or investment to make the decision. According to the realtor, scare tactics are employed to urge locals to sell their houses because "those people" are moving into the region, causing them to panic. People who belong to a different creed, race, or ethnic group from the one in issue are referred to as "those people."

Blockbusting is a cynical method used to generate real estate listings and profits for real estate agents and/or investors. It preys on people's biases and anxieties to generate listings and revenues. It also has the effect of pushing prices down, which may increase overall sales volume. Real estate brokers who influence or guide buyers or renters away from a certain community may be able to steer them away from a specific community if they are members of a protected class.

The tactic was popular during the civil rights era and was utilized by the housing sector (together with blockbusting) to dissuade African Americans from living in mostly white neighborhoods. Followers of other ethnic and religious groups, as well as families with young children, are also barred from visiting particular locations or residential buildings, as is the case with members of the Muslim faith. Although there is a beneficial aspect to steering, there is also a bad aspect. If a potential buyer specifies that they only want to see houses in specified neighborhoods based on their race, religion, or ethnic group, the seller will honor the request. A real estate agent who agrees to this request is engaged in guiding and, as a result, is violating the law. It is recommended that the buyer create a nondiscriminatory wish list that will be utilized to choose the homes that will be presented to them during the showing process.

This strategy has nothing to do with the loan industry. It is the strategy of banks to refuse to grant loans and mortgages to individuals who reside in specific neighborhoods and restrict the amount of money they may lend to them in such communities. In metropolitan locations, especially inner cities, these types of communities are common occurrences. In addition to the content in an advertisement, it is possible that the images may be problematic as well. According to the National Fair Housing Alliance, the Fair Housing Act prohibits the use of models in media that are targeted at a specific racial or national origin group without a parallel campaign aimed at other groups. A strong prohibition is also placed on using models to suggest that only adults are permitted to enter a certain property or that only one sex is permitted to enter. Similarly, the place where an advertisement is shown is regulated by HUD laws.

Displaying billboards, leaflets, or newspaper advertisements that are intended to be seen by just specific segments of the population, for example, is strictly prohibited. A prohibition is also placed on the practice of distributing property announcements and displays to just a select number of brokers.

The fair housing insignia on any promotional materials other than those that explicitly promote fair housing is not authorized under the Fair Housing Act. If a realtor fails to put the insignia on an advertisement and then sends a customer to a house that violates the fair housing act, the realtor will be the subject of a lawsuit against the realtor. Local, state, and federal governments have passed fair housing legislation to guarantee that fair housing regulations are implemented. State laws may be more or less strict than federal law in terms of protected groups and prohibited activity, and in a court of law, the legislation that is found to be more rigorous would be enforced.

On the other hand, there may be no state or municipal legislation that conflicts with federal law. In this case, for example, no local legislation that authorizes redlining would be found to be legally legitimate under the United States Constitution.

Before taking the exam, it is vital that you research and become acquainted with the standards of your state and municipal fair housing laws. You may use the federal law as a starting point for drawing comparisons with other states' legislation.

Public land-use laws

In accordance with the United States Constitution, the federal government has the jurisdiction to regulate the use of the private property. This authority is one of the police powers assigned to the federal government by the Constitution. However, even though "police powers" appear to be sinister, as if big brother is always looking over your shoulder, the purpose of police powers is to regulate the behavior of its residents for the common good, which includes the general welfare, order and safety of the general public, among other things. If a state building code requires that a bedroom have a window, a slumlord may opt to flout that requirement by permitting tenants to place illegal barriers and locks to gather more money from desperate people. Not only does this go counter to the state construction law, but it also runs against the state fire code, which specifies the maximum number of people that may be safely accommodated in a structure.

In large cities and in the great majority of municipalities, zoning regulations exist, except for Houston, Texas. Those who possess land and property are subject to these restrictions, limiting how they may utilize their land and property. Zones are the most often used kind of zoning, and they divide a city or town into geographic pieces, with each sector designated for a certain function. Examples include two kinds of residential zones (single-family and multifamily), as well as industrial and commercial zones, among other classifications, in a municipality. Only specified types of buildings may be constructed inside specific zones, and as a consequence, only specific types of uses may be authorized within those zones. A "mixed-use zone," which would include businesses such as convenience stores, dry cleaners, and other such companies in addition to offices and residences, is also a possibility in the future. In addition to its intended use, zoning regulations may also govern the size of lots and setbacks, the square footage of buildings, and the height of structures. An owner may be denied permission to build a shed for the storage of tools, or their ability to build a shed may be limited based on the severity of the zoning restriction. Variations in zoning allow for a degree of adjustability in the design.

Take, for example, the case of a developer who is denied permission to build because of a zoning restriction; the developer may be eligible for relief by filing an application for a variance to the local Zoning Board of Adjustment. To submit their case before the zoning board in a public hearing, the developer would have to appear before the board in person. A quasi-judicial institution that makes judgments on land use and development, the zoning board, is similar to the planning board in its function. The applicant may invite witnesses, some of whom are experts in their fields, to testify on their behalf.

Questions from members of the general public are accepted for each of these experts. It is also possible for the attorney representing any objectors who have acquired legal representation to cross-examine the witnesses on their behalf. In addition to witnesses and members of the general public, objectors and members of the general public may be asked to testify. After presenting their evidence, they are susceptible to cross-examination by the applicant or by the applicant's counsel. The public is invited to offer comments under oath after completing both sides' arguments. These comments will be included in the official record of the proceedings, which is the zoning board meeting, which will be published.

In accordance with local zoning regulations, state land-use laws, and precedent, the zoning board grants or refuses the applicant's variance request after taking all relevant factors into account. It is necessary to meet certain prerequisites when filing for an exemption, both favorably and negatively, before the exemption may be granted. In general, an area variance is a variation from zoning restrictions that refers to the size of a yard or lot, the floor area ratio, or the height of a building. Think about the situation of a homeowner who wants to build an addition to their garage. This is because, due to its unique topography, the expansion would be closer to the street than is authorized by the zoning law. For a property owner to be qualified for an area variance, they must meet a variety of positive and negative standards, both positive and negative in nature.

To fulfill the affirmative requirements of the application, the petitioner must establish that the property's shape generates extraordinary practical challenges or excessive hardship or that a one-of-a-kind event happens that influences the particular property. The applicant must establish that granting the variance would not be considerably detrimental to the public good or that it would not significantly undermine the goal and purpose of the zoning plan and zoning regulations under the negative criteria.

An applicant must establish that the variance application is for a specific piece of real estate and that the adoption of the variance would promote the aims of the land use laws to get a variance from one kind of zoning to another type of zoning. Applicants for variances must demonstrate that the grant of the variance will not result in a significant detriment to the public good, that the benefits will outweigh any negative consequences, and that the grant of a variance will not substantially impair the intent and purpose of the zone plan and zoning ordinance on the negative side. A use variance is an exception provided when use is legal in one zone but not in another, as is the case in question.

For example, a property owner who intends to convert an empty space above the garage into a rental apartment may apply to the local government for a variance to allow the conversion. In order to be approved, the use must be assessed to be fundamentally beneficial to the property or specifically adapted to the specific property. Taking into consideration that one of the positive requirements has been met, one of the negative criteria must also be met, which means that it must be demonstrated that the variance will not result in significant harm to the public good or that it will not significantly undermine the existing planning and zoning regulations. Application for a special use permit is a request for a departure from existing regulations to introduce a use that is not authorized in the region where the permit is being requested. Consider the scenario in which a charter school intends to convert a mansion into a school. A judgment by the zoning board would be based on many factors, including the proposed use's compatibility with the surrounding neighborhood, public testimony or other evidence submitted in response to the request, and the proposed use's compliance with the general objective of the zoning code. An application for a special use permit is also known as a conditional use permit, a conditional use approval, or a special use variance, depending on the context in which it is issued.

Some further variables may need the use of use variances if a property owner decides to make modifications to their land. It is referred to as a nonconforming use when an activity or structure is out of character with the surrounding region and occurs before introducing zoning laws and rules.

Nonconforming use

A variance is only required if the property owner seeks to expand the size of the nonconforming construction or change the use of the structure. When a fuel station was constructed before the zoning code was formed and is situated where people live, the owner may decide to include a service area for vehicles experiencing mechanical troubles. Consequently, the owner would be expanding his nonconforming use, and as a result, he would need a use variance from the municipality.

Accessory construction

Examine the case where a property owner is banned from developing an outbuilding for storage because of an existing zoning restriction. During a public hearing, the property owner may be required to present their case for or against the zoning variance requested by the zoning board of appeals. It is the same set of requirements for a use variance as it is for any other kind of use variance. Customers may drop off and pick up their cleaning without having to park their cars and enter the facility, as in the case of a dry cleaner. This is an illustration of the use of an accessory. Even though it is not the usual manner of customer communication with a dry cleaner, it is advantageous to the dry cleaner's business.

For a site plan assessment, the dry cleaner would have to appear before the planning board; nevertheless, it is likely that they would not need a variance. If, on the other hand, the dry cleaner's accessory use is forbidden by the zoning code, the dry cleaner would be needed to apply to the zoning board for approval of a use variance based on the conditions for that kind of exemption to continue operating.

Historically, cities were still in the process of developing and expanding. After the United States joined World War I in 1917, municipalities did not begin to adopt zoning restrictions until the early twentieth century. Then there were the master plans, which were meticulously drawn out. It is a long-range plan for the area containing a certain political unit, such as a city, town, or region, developed with an intended end goal in mind. Master planning may be defined as follows: The master plan is designed with a single purpose in mind, and it is then examined regularly once it has been completed.

A community vision statement expresses what the local government unit, in collaboration with the people, feels is the most desirable development for the future of the town or city, or maybe the whole region. Numerous elements are included in the design, including housing, transit networks, public utilities, open spaces, and economic development. Writing and implementing zoning laws that are compatible with the recommendations of the master plan are two of how a municipality may bring its master plan to fruition and bring it into reality. Density zoning, downzoning, inclusionary zoning, and cluster zoning are all strategies that are being used in different states and municipalities to solve specific concerns such as population growth, affordable housing shortages, and availability of affordable housing.

Generalization: The number of residences that may be built on an acre of land is referred to as the density zoning of a neighborhood. It is being used in rural areas where farmers are selling their land to developers to earn cash to supplement their existing income. By establishing this kind of zoning law, communities may control growth in these rural areas while at the same time offering help to farmers. Farmers who want to maximize the value of their land assets should consider selling a portion of their land to a developer who will be able to build more homes on smaller lots while making as much money (at least theoretically) as they would if they were selling larger lots with larger residences on them. The farmer will be granted the right to keep a piece of the land for agricultural purposes for his efforts.

Generally speaking, downzoning is the practice of reducing the amount of density or use authorized on a parcel of land. Consider this scenario: An area is zoned to allow for apartment complexes with 400 units, but a government agency (not the zoning board) is concerned about densification issues and alters the zoning to allow for structures with 250 units. Inclusionary zoning, which is used to ensure that low- and moderate-income housing is included in new housing developments such as apartment complexes and subdivisions, targets low- and moderate-income housing for inclusion. The term "affordable housing" is also used to describe it.

For the percentage of affordable housing units to market-rate flats, a predetermined ratio has been established, and developers are required to adhere to this ratio. Depending on the land use designation, a planned unit development (PUD) may include various types of land uses, including residential, commercial, and even industrial land uses. There is additional open space on the land, which has been designated as such. When it comes to land use, cluster zoning is a word that describes how different types of land use are clustered or grouped together in certain geographic places. In real estate, a subdivision is a large piece of land divided into smaller lots, each of which will be used to build new houses.

Similar to the majority of other areas of real estate, zoning regulations controlling subdivisions are different from one state to another. In most cases, however, the tract owner must submit a plat with the local planning commission, which is a map specifying the size and location of individual lots, roadways, electricity lines, and any communal structures or facilities, such as a clubhouse or swimming pool.

Those involved in the planning of subdivisions are responsible for adhering strictly to all relevant zoning restrictions in terms of lot sizes and the construction of buildings inside the subdivision. If the site is sold to other homebuilders or individual homeowners after the initial development, the developer who initially created the land is responsible for adhering to any applicable zoning requirements on the land. As an example, a developer would be obliged to submit to the appropriate planning board for examination and approval a request to divide land before any construction could commence on the project. Any homeowner who intends to subdivide their property into two or more lots must follow the steps outlined in this document.

Eminent domain is the term used to describe the taking of property by a unit of government, whether federal, state, or municipal, for the purpose of public use. This category includes various uses, including highways, open space, urban regeneration, and public housing, to name a few. Besides public utilities such as electric companies, the power of eminent domain may be employed by individuals to acquire land for their own benefit.

State and local laws control the taking of property for any cause, and property owners must be reimbursed at the fair market worth of their property in order to avoid civil liability. Once the property has been assessed, the value of the property may be calculated. For example, a city may engage in discussions with property owners in order to purchase land for the construction of a new bridge. Those property owners who believe that the assessed value reflects fair market value choose to accept the city's offer and depart their residences immediately. The offer is rejected by a tiny proportion of property owners. They may be able to prevent the city from taking possession of their land via a legal procedure known as condemnation, which is a legal process. If the city is successful in its attempts, the landowners will still be compensated for their land at the fair market value that the city determined at the time of purchase. Assume that the approach will take up two and a half blocks of real estate in the city. Those who own property on the remaining half-block may also ask the city to acquire their homes, noting the harmful effect that the additional traffic and noise will have on their quality of life as justification. As a result, it is referred to as inverse condemnation in this situation. The Interstate Land Sales Full Disclosure Act (ILS), a federal legislation, governs land transactions across state boundaries. According to the Department of Housing and Urban Development, the act applies to certain kinds of subdivisions and is enforced by the agency (HUD).

A land developer is obliged to register with the Department of Housing and Urban Development (HUD) and provide a property report to each potential buyer prior to completing the purchase agreement. Customers are safeguarded against deceptive practices in interstate land sales and leasing under the terms of this Act. Typically, vacation homes and condos sell at a high rate, and state regulations restrict these types of transactions. All of these items are needed to be included in an accurate legal description of the subdivision, as well as a map, a statement of the status of the title to the land in the subdivision, and a declaration of the fundamental terms and conditions for selling or leasing lots in the subdivision.

The developer must provide copies of the developer's articles of incorporation, trust agreements or partnership agreement, and the property report, depending on the kind of corporate structure under which the developer is organized. It is necessary to attach an addendum to the report that contains copies of both the subdivision deed and any easements or limits that may be applicable. While the information about a property must be included in the property report, the documentation that goes with it is not required. They are now on file with the Department of Housing and Urban Development and may be obtained for a nominal fee by contacting them directly. Those documents, as well as others, are specified in the Act and are needed as part of the registration package that must be submitted to the Department of Housing and Urban Development by the developer (HUD).

Understanding Federal Fair Housing Laws

Whether they are brokers or salespeople, real estate agents in each state are expected to be knowledgeable with and comply with the fair housing laws in their respective jurisdictions. Property agents play a significant role in the promotion of fair housing and the avoidance of prejudice in the residential real estate industry and in the community at large. Because fair housing standards apply to all parts of the country, including your state, state exam designers assume that you will be acquainted with fair housing requirements at the federal level, which they have included in their preparation. Fair housing regulations have been adopted by a large number of states, counties, and municipalities, which are in addition to federal fair housing laws. State examiners assume that you will be conversant with the relevant local law that is being tested on your behalf. As you study for the state licensing exam, you should be familiar with the fair housing standards that apply in your state or local jurisdiction. In this chapter, I explain the restrictions that the federal government has adopted to ban discrimination in the sale and rental of real estate, including land, houses, apartment complexes, and hiring employees. In the United States, these federal fair housing rules are comprised of a collection of distinct acts that have been enacted at various times throughout history. I also go over the groups that are protected by these laws (referred to as protected classes), as well as the specific discriminatory actions that are forbidden by these laws (referred to as prohibited activities). Finally, you will find information on how the law is enforced and a few exceptions to the norm to complete your educational experience.

Overall, fair housing rules are meant to outlaw discrimination in housing while also providing people the opportunity to live where they wish on a level playing field. Federal, state, and municipal fair housing legislation are in place to achieve this goal at the federal, state, and local levels. As a previous student of mine pointed out, monetary discrimination is the only kind of discrimination that is permissible under law. It wasn't that long ago that a fair housing advertisement said unequivocally that the only color that could be discriminated against was the color green, as in money green. Capitalism is symbolized by the color red in the United States of America. In this section, I intend to go over certain federal legislation that deals with housing discrimination and some crucial dates that you should keep in mind as you go through this section. I also intend to present a fascinating case in which it has been shown that a law is still a law regardless of how long it has been in force. In addition, I address state and local rules and the all-important fair housing poster, which you can get for free from this website. When you are a broker who hires persons, you must also be aware of and comply with anti-discrimination standards that apply to the recruitment process and any other applicable laws.

Generally speaking, equal employment regulations are not taught in real estate courses and are only seldom examined in real estate examinations. However, this is changing. In contrast, if you're thinking about applying for a broker's license, you should check whether your state's exam requires you to know anything about equal opportunity employment standards, especially regarding recruitment methods. United States real estate agents are primarily concerned with and accountable for implementing federal fair housing laws. In this section, I offer you the knowledge of a sufficient number of federal legislations. I can nearly guarantee that you will meet a few questions about these statutes on the exam. Chapter 15 concludes with a description of another set of legislation associated with fair housing. The financing of real estate is covered in that chapter. The rules I discuss there focus on providing equal opportunity and information throughout the critical mortgage loan application process.

It was soon after the end of the American Civil War in 1866 that the Civil Rights Act of 1866 was passed by the United States This legislation prohibits discrimination based on race or color in the purchase, sale, lease, or conveyance of real property (including real estate and personal property). Although the wording of the Act is plain in the sense that it effectively asserts that all citizens, regardless of race, shall be entitled to the same property rights, it does not include any exceptions. The second distinctive element of the legislation is that it enables for the performance of enforcement actions by taking the subject immediately before a federal court of law.

However, an important 1968 court case based on the act resulted in a landmark fair housing law decision that is being used as a model for other courts today. The United States Supreme Court rendered its ruling in Jones v. Alfred H. Mayer Company, in which it mainly ruled that the 1866 Act prohibited any discrimination against people of color by private individuals or the government, with no exceptions. This lawsuit was filed against the city of Chicago after the passage of the Fair Housing Act in 1968 in the United States. Even though there are no exceptions to the 1866 Act, the lack of any exceptions is noteworthy since more recent fair housing laws do, in fact, include exceptions to several elements.

It is still considered legal today, partly since it was the first act passed and is still in effect. The 1866 legislation has been upheld in the Jones vs Mayer case, which found that it outperformed subsequent statutes in terms of exceptions for discrimination based on race. Racial discrimination in housing is illegal in all 50 states and the District of Columbia. The Fair Housing Act of 1968 is formally known as Title VIII (sometimes written "Title Eight") of the Civil Rights Act of 1968 (also known as the Fair Housing Act of 1968). (Also spelled "Title Eight"). This law, which was the first of its kind in the twentieth century, prohibited certain behaviors that were deemed to be discriminatory in relation to housing and the expressly designated groups, known as protected classes, to whom it applied. It was the first act of its kind in the twentieth century. There were no specific exclusions, in contrast to the Civil Rights Act of 1866 (which was addressed in the prior section). The 1968 Fair Housing Act, along with other landmark civil rights legislation from 1866 to 1974, and the 1988 Fair Housing Amendments Act expanded the scope of existing protections to include even more protected classes.

These landmark laws serve as the foundation for fair housing standards as they apply to real estate agents. In 1968, Congress passed the Housing and Urban Development Act, which is now enforced by the Department of Housing and Urban Development (HUD). This legislation may be broken down into three categories: what you can't do (prohibited activities), what you can't do (protected groups), and exceptions to the rule. In this way, I can incorporate this information into the rest of the chapter's overall structure and organization. Check out "Don't Do It: Avoiding Discriminatory Actions," "Feeling Safe: Identifying Who Is Protected," and "Bending the Rules: Understanding Exceptions to the Law" for further resources.

In recent years, state and local governments, such as counties and cities, have adopted progressive fair housing legislation. As a consequence, these municipal laws must be studied and followed alongside federal fair housing legislation, rather than in place of it, and their rights must be recognized. When federal and local laws cover the same subject matter, the rule of thumb is that the more restrictive or harder legislation will take priority over the legislation that is less restrictive or rougher.

Unlike local restrictions, which sometimes do not cover prohibited conduct, federal legislation, on the other hand, is rather comprehensive in terms of forbidding discriminatory activity. Other protected groups or organizations that need protection under the fair housing laws are periodically added in municipal housing ordinances that are enacted on a case-by-case basis. Several cities and at least one state, for example, have included sexual orientation as a protected class under their fair housing laws, which is the first time this has happened in the United States. On top of that, exceptions to the rule of law that are authorized under federal law are sometimes removed at the state and local levels. Whenever convicted sexual offenders are released from prison and relocate to a new region, Megan's Law provides an incentive for them to register with the local police department. According to the official website, it was put into effect by the federal government in 2009. Because of Megan's Law, there have been raised problems concerning the civil rights and privacy rights of offenders in local authorities, as well as the rights of victims in certain situations.

Consult with your state's licensing authorities to learn more about your responsibilities as an agent, which include providing prospective buyers with information regarding the presence of sex offenders in the area. In addition, see Chapter 4 for further details.

In order to study for the exam and, more importantly, to prepare for your future real estate career, you must explore and understand as much as you can about any local, state, or municipal policies that complement federal fair housing requirements. Keep a careful eye out for any more prohibited activities, additional protected groups, or exceptions to the exclusions that may have been introduced after your initial assessment and make note of them. Designed by the Department of Housing and Urban Development (HUD), which is in charge of implementing the Federal Fair Housing Act, the poster must be prominently displayed in all real estate offices. The poster is available for download here. When a complaint is made against a real estate agent, the omission to display the sign may be seen as a breach of fair housing regulations and may be used as evidence of discrimination against the complainant.

The Department of Housing and Urban Development (HUD) also requires that its fair housing emblem or other appropriate language be used in all real estate advertising, including newspaper and magazine ads. According to the Federal Fair Housing Act of 1968, the essential parts define various activities that are regarded discriminatory and prohibit them from occurring in the housing market.

I am not familiar with the legislative history that led to the passage of this legislation, but from what I have read, it appears that Congress wanted to discourage those who might try to split hairs in their irrational efforts to circumvent a statute that clearly states, "Do not discriminate," from attempting to do so. This has resulted in a list of particular actions being included into the legislative framework. For each duty that is listed, I go through everything in-depth and provide examples for each one that is discussed.

Please keep in mind that these tactics are considered to be discriminatory in the housing market and are, as a result, not allowed. Check your understanding and recollection of prohibited activities, as well as your understanding and recall of how to spot them if they are provided in questions that incorporate short case studies, before taking the exam. Real estate agents in each state, regardless of whether they are brokers or salespeople, are obliged to be educated about and to adhere to the fair housing legislation in their respective jurisdictions, whether they are brokers or salespeople. The promotion of fair housing and the prevention of bias in the residential real estate sector, as well as in the broader society, are important goals for real estate brokers to strive towards.

Because fair housing regulations apply across the nation, including your own state, state test designers anticipate that you will be familiar with fair housing requirements at the federal level, which they have incorporated in their preparation for the exam. In addition to federal fair housing legislation, a vast number of states, counties, and municipalities have established fair housing standards, which are in addition to federal fair housing laws. According to the results of state tests, you will be required to know the appropriate local legislation.

Chapter 6: Environmental Laws

Realtors need to be aware of any potential health risks when it comes time to promote a property or, if they are not the listing agent, when it comes time to show a house to prospective buyers. Real estate brokers are responsible for informing sellers of their legal duties under various laws, such as the Lead Paint Disclosure Act, as well as buyers of their legal rights under any laws related to hazardous substances. Any past or present environmental dangers in the area, such as a polluted flow from runoff from a chemical plant further upriver (even if the pollution has been cleaned up), or the presence of an operating nuclear power plant, are all subject to the responsibility of a realtor to be knowledgeable about such hazards. If you read the definition of a "hazardous material," often known as a "hazmat," you will find that it differs depending on every government agency you consult. A total of four federal agencies are responsible for regulating hazardous materials: the Environmental Protection Agency (EPA), OSHA, the Department of Transportation (DOT), and the Nuclear Regulatory Commission (NRC). The Environmental Protection Agency is responsible for environmental protection, occupational safety and health, and occupational safety and health (NRC). Nuclear materials and their by-products are regulated by the National Nuclear Security Administration, which is under the supervision of the Department of Transportation for the safe transportation of hazardous goods. Except in the event of a hazardous materials spill occurring on or near a property or a nuclear power station being located nearby, these two agencies are not of concern to us. In certain cases, however, they are.

When it comes to hazardous materials, the Environmental Protection Agency (EPA) blends the description of what hazardous materials are capable of doing with the notion of how hazardous materials enter the environment, which was created by the Occupational Safety and Health Administration (OSHA) (OSHA). Hazardous materials, according to the Institute of Hazardous Materials Management, are defined as "any health or physical hazard that is toxic to humans, toxic, or corrosive, or that acts on different parts of the body, animal, or plant," and that can enter the environment "through spilling, leaking, pumping, pouring, emitting, emptying, discharging, dumping, or disposing of." Hazardous materials (hamates) are classified by the Environmental Protection Agency (EPA) into more than 350 distinct categories, which might manifest themselves as "dusts, gases, fumes, vapors, mists, or smoke." The presence of some health hazards, such as smoke blowing from a nearby industrial site, will be immediately apparent to a prospective buyer, who will direct the realtor to continue driving, but other potential health concerns will be more difficult to detect. Despite the fact that lead, asbestos, radon, and mound are not always visible, the presence of mound may be identified via the sense of taste.

You may be asked questions on any of the subjects listed below during the exam. Prior to the invention of acrylic paint, lead was a key component, and it is still used today. In 1978, the FDA banned its use owing to the toxicity of the substance, which was especially dangerous in children under the age of six. People are exposed to lead by inhalation of lead dust, which has been demonstrated to affect the neurological system, kidneys, and reproductive systems. Research suggests that lead poisoning may also result in signs and symptoms of attention deficit disorder (ADD) and attention deficit hyperactivity disorder (ADHD) (ADHD).

Owners of homes built before 1978 are obligated to disclose the presence of lead paint in their dwellings or flats to potential purchasers and renters under the terms of the Residential Lead-Based Paint Hazard Reduction Act, which was signed into law in 1992 and became effective in 1993. Buyers and tenants should be provided with a copy of the government pamphlet Protect Your Family from Lead in Your Home, which should be sent at the time of contract signing by both the seller and landlord. In the next ten days, the buyer can arrange for testing to determine whether or not there is lead present in the home. Despite the fact that it is optional, the Environmental Protection Agency recommends it, especially if little children are involved.

In certain instances, lead-based paint inspections or risk assessments are carried out, while in others, a lead hazard screen is utilized to identify potential hazards. For a long time, certain building materials included asbestos, a mineral fiber used to increase heat absorption and fire resistance, among other things. Other applications for the material included pipe and furnace duct insulation, as well as a soundproofing material, in addition to siding and roofing. Asbestos is a carcinogen that may cause lung cancer and asbestosis, which is a lung condition in its own right. The Environmental Protection Agency (EPA) began limiting the use of asbestos in specified goods in 1989, citing the possibility that asbestos might cause lung cancer and asbestosis. The scope of the restriction has been broadened to include a wide variety of building materials as well as many other industries.

For the most part, asbestos is not a problem in and of itself. Because of its brittleness, or the tendency to dissolve, it is a subject of concern. When asbestos begins to break down or is disturbed during a building repair, a small quantity of asbestos is discharged into the air, and humans and animals may inhale these particles. When asbestos is in good condition, it is not required to remove the material completely. An well-versed expert in the correct removal procedures should be hired to remove it if a property owner wants it gone. Any asbestos-related repair work carried out on a property by an unskilled person should be notified to and recorded by the property owner as soon as it is discovered.

Instead of removing the asbestos, it may be sufficient to have it encapsulated or otherwise shielded from environmental exposure. Both methods bind or coat asbestos fibers with sealant; however, the former does not utilize any sealant. It is confined inside the enclosure to prevent asbestos exposure. In the United States, it is the second most common cause of lung cancer after smoking, and it is very dangerous. Additionally, it is radioactive and lacks any discernible odor, taste, or smell. It exists in nature due to the decomposition of rocks and soil, and it is created as a by-product of the degradation of the same materials.

Radon may be found in all regions of the United States (and the world). It is most often seen on lower levels, like in a basement or cellar. Radon testing should thus be carried out at the lowest possible level of a building that will be used as a residential area as a consequence of this.

According to the Environmental Protection Agency and the Surgeon General of the United States, Sellers should get their homes tested before putting them on the market. They also recommend that all buyers inquire if radon testing has been completed and, if so, get a copy of the testing results before making a purchase. If the seller has not had a radon test done, the Environmental Protection Agency and the Surgeon General recommend that the buyer get one done as soon as possible. Buyers who want to have radon testing done may do it either before or after the contract is signed, depending on their preferences. However, it is necessary to specify in the contract that, if the testing is performed later, the sale of the residence is contingent upon the buyer's satisfaction, which may be set by law, with the results of the testing.

When it comes to radon testing, there are a range of options. To begin, a charcoal canister is placed in a dwelling for a certain period of time before being transported to a laboratory for examination. In order to be effective, the other ways must be used in combination with a device or detector that continuously monitors radon levels over a prolonged period. Several states and municipalities require radon mitigation, even though the Environmental Protection Agency (EPA) does not mandate it. Increased ventilation in problem regions may assist in lowering the amount of radon in the surrounding environment.

A growing number of people who suffer from severe allergies are becoming more concerned about mound growth in their homes. Mold is a microscopic fungus that produces spores that may cause allergic reactions in humans. Mold is a kind of fungus that has the potential to trigger allergic responses in people. Mold may grow in wet conditions, so keep an eye out for it. An elevated mound may begin to develop in the affected region when a leak occurs between the ceiling of a bathroom on one level and the ceiling of a closet on the floor below.

It is acknowledged by the Environmental Protection Agency (EPA) that there is "no practicable means to remove all of the mound and mound spores from the interior environment" and that there are currently no

EPA mound standards or recommendations in effect. The Environmental Protection Agency (EPA) does recommend that "the most effective way to reduce indoor mound growth is to regulate moisture," according to their recommendations. To prevent moisture from forming in their homes, the Environmental Protection Agency recommends that homeowners take the following steps: repair plumbing leaks and seepage into basements from the ground, use dehumidifiers and air conditioners to remove moisture from the air, and install insulation on storm windows to prevent moisture from forming. Alternatively, any indication of a mound will be eliminated by a clever merchant on time.

The vast majority of people get their water via privately owned water firms or publicly controlled water utilities. The federal Safe Drinking Water Act (SDWA) of 1974 demands that the public's water supply be tested on a regular basis to ensure that it is safe to drink, despite the fact that none of these areas are immune from the development of water-borne diseases. Those who have private wells that serve less than 25 people are at a higher risk of contaminating their water supply. There are no rules in place for them under the SDWA. Whether there is a private well on the property, and whether wastes are disposed of by an onsite sewage system, septic system, or cesspool should be disclosed to a prospective buyer.

Private well

Unless you are dealing with rural properties, you will have a difficult time locating a private well these days, unless you are lucky. According to the most current estimates, private wells offer drinking water to just around ten percent of the country's population. According to the Environmental Protection Agency, well water should be tested once a year. It is possible to test wells for lead, radon, and the presence of chemicals from fertilizer and pesticide runoff, among other potentially hazardous compounds. The septic system and the cesspool are two different things. When there is no sewer infrastructure to convey waste to a central sewage treatment plant as rapidly as possible, these are techniques for disposing of human waste. A septic system consists of two parts: a large tank that collects sewage from the residence and a leaching area where the sewage is cleaned before being released back into the environment. In a holding tank, once bacteria have cleaned the wastes, the liquid component of the waste is released into a leach field, also known as an absorption field, where it is absorbed into the ground.

A percolation test, also known as a perk test, should be requested by a prospective buyer to establish the feasibility of installing and maintaining a septic system and the costs associated with doing so. A buyer may request that the seller have the tank pumped as a condition of the sale, depending on the quantity of sludge that has accumulated in the tank. While a cesspool works in the same manner as an ordinary septic system, it does not need a leaching field since the treated liquid flows directly from the tank into the dirt around the tank rather than into the surrounding ground.

A prospective buyer should be provided with the same information about a cesspool as they would be provided with information about a sewage disposal system. As you can see, if a septic system or a cesspool is not designed and maintained correctly, they both have the potential to cause harm to well water as well as the land around them. It is also possible that groundwater pollution is generated by underground storage tanks that are not adequately sealed (USTs). Additionally, more information about USTs may be found in the section after this one. A realtor should be aware of environmental dangers such as brownfields, underground storage tanks, and landfills. Environmental problems connected to brownfields, underground storage tanks, and landfills may be covered in detail on the examination. Real estate agents should be aware of any of the following conditions in the context of the property they are selling and/or displaying. The possibility of lead poisoning in the soil exists in addition to the threats provided by hazardous wastes that may leak into water sources, be thrown into the atmosphere, or seep into the ground. While repainting your home, it's possible that the lead paint on the outside of your home may be scraped off. According to the Environmental Protection Agency, a brownfield is described as "abandoned or unused properties whose rehabilitation or expansion may be hampered by possible environmental pollution," according to the Environmental Protection Agency. The majority of these properties were formerly utilized as commercial or industrial establishments. As estimated by the Environmental Protection Agency, the United States has between 500,000 and 1 million brownfields. Small Business Liability Relief and Brownfields Revitalization Act of 2002 and the Comprehensive Environmental Response, Compensation, and Liability Act of 1980 (CERCLA) are all laws that regulate the revitalization of brownfields (SBLRBRA). According to CERCLA, the chemical and petroleum companies were charged to support cleanup activities at brownfield sites, which served as the cornerstone for the Superfund program. As part of its regulatory framework, CERCLA created procedures for dealing with closed and abandoned hazardous waste sites and liability provisions for persons liable for the discharge of hazardous material at these locations. CERCLA defines responsibility in two ways: as either strict liability or as joint and several liabilities, depending on the circumstances. Under strict liability, the property owner is held liable regardless of whether or not the owner was at fault for the circumstances. Joint and several obligations refer to the fact that any and all owners, including prior owners, are jointly and severally liable for their actions. Every one is liable in the event of a legal action.

If a party is found liable and only one of the owners, for example, has the financial means to pay the judgment, the money required to fulfill the judgment will come from that party. This is true despite the fact that the judgment was rendered against all of the owners. For this reason, environmental indemnification clauses are incorporated in all commercial real estate transactions, including mortgage deals. According to the Superfund Act, the amount of money available in the Superfund increased from $1.6 billion to $8.5 billion, plus an extra $500 million for cleaning underground oil tanks that had leaked into the environment.

Additionally, provisions of the act emphasize the importance of permanent remedies and the use of new technologies in the cleanup of toxic and radioactive waste sites, increase the involvement of states in Superfund programmers, establish an open-records provision for information about the use and release of hazardous chemicals into the environment, and encourage increased community participation in site cleanup decisions. The act also provides protection to innocent landowners, a safeguard known as innocent landowner immunity, in addition to the other provisions.

Even though the current owner of the property had nothing to do with the prior production or disposal of hazardous waste, they were deemed accountable under CERCLA and were required to pay for the cleaning of the site. According to the SARA, if the current owner had a Phase I environmental assessment conducted at the time of the sale and no hazardous substances were detected (even though they were there), the current owner would not be responsible for any site cleaning expenditures. As a result of the SBLRBRA, the classes of individuals protected from responsibility have been expanded to include those engaged in certain real estate transactions, and the term "innocent landowner" has been defined. The Act also improves state brownfields programmers and makes financial assistance for brownfield rehabilitation projects more readily accessible to developers.

Basic Requirements for a Valid Contract

When two or more people agree to do or not do anything, they have entered into a legally binding agreement that is enforceable under the laws of the nation in which the agreement was established. Agreements for the representation of a buyer or the listing of a property are legally enforceable contracts. Deeds are legal papers that provide a person the legal right to possess property and act as documentation of that legal right to possess property. Deeds are used to transfer ownership of property from one person to another. This right of possession, which is often referred to as ownership, is included in the title to the property.

Contracts serve as the starting point for the selling and purchase process, and the transfer of ownership of the property via the signing of the deed puts the process to an end. It is essential for real estate agents to understand the terms of contracts and deeds. There will, without a doubt, be a number of questions on the exam that will be relevant to their field of expertise.

Parties in a position of authority

Everyone who enters into a contract must be legally competent, which means they must be aware of and comprehend all of the conditions of the agreement they are about to enter. They must be at least the legal drinking age in their respective states; they must not be mentally challenged or mentally ill. They must not have been subjected to improper influence, pressure, or misrepresentation by another, and they must not be under the influence of alcohol or drugs. When a property is owned by tenants in common, one of the parties has the right to sell their half of the property, even if the other party is unable or unwilling to sell their share of the asset.

Both parties must agree on the terms and conditions that will be used to carry out the transaction before it can be formalized into a legal agreement. This criterion is referred to as the offer and acceptance requirement, the reality of consent requirement, mutual assent, mutual agreement, and the meeting of the mind's requirement, among other terms and phrases. This criterion also means that the contract's wording should be basic and easy to understand. One strategy for getting out of a contract is claiming that the contract's wording was ambiguous in order to claim that they did not understand what was being said in it. For a contract to be lawful, the motivation for entering into it must be genuine.

Unlawful purposes would result in a contract being declared null and void, which means that it would be considered as if it had never been signed in the first place. An application for and receipt of a mortgage on one property, but with the intention of using the funds of that mortgage contract to support the purchase of another property, results in a null and void mortgage transaction on that property. It is important to remember that for a contract to be legal, the contractual parties must exchange benefits (i.e., something of value). A real estate transaction is completed when money is passed from the buyer to the seller in exchange for property, and this occurs at the moment of transfer of money from one party to another (the selling price). It is only after the payment of commissions that the agreements between real estate brokers and principals come to an end (or brings them to a close).Leases are a kind of contract in which rent (money) must be paid in exchange for ownership of a rental unit. The lease is also a type of contract in which consideration for the renter's payment of rent is taken into account (money). A contract must be written in order to be valid. State laws regarding the need for a written contract in a real estate transaction vary, but in general, such contracts must be completed in written form to be valid. A written contract is always a good idea, regardless of whether a written contract is needed by law. This ensures that all parties are aware of what they are agreeing to. When everyone engaged knows the boundaries of the agreement, it is also easier to discuss the conditions. Listings must be filed in writing in all states, regardless of the jurisdiction. In this case, rather than being subject to the Statute of Frauds, employment agreements are governed by the real estate licensing regulations.

Several examples are provided below to aid you in sifting through these seemingly similar but fundamentally different legal concepts about contracts. A genuine contract comprises all five characteristics described above, and it is legally enforceable in court. A contract may have additional qualities depending on the reason for which it is being used, but the five characteristics stated above are always included in a legally binding agreement. It is possible to enforce a legally binding contract. The buyer may be able to sue the seller to force them to sell the property if, after signing a contract to sell their property, they decide not to sell it. Based on the circumstances, a court would very probably decide in favor of the buyer; yet, in reality, the buyer would almost surely accept monetary damages. According to the reasoning presented, a legally binding contract may be enforced in a court of law. As a general rule, the statute of limitations, the passage of time, or the doctrine of estoppel may all make even a legally binding contract unenforceable. The statute of limitations is a legal term limiting the length of time a person has to pursue a legal action against another party. The time period begins when the action is first performed. Depending on the state, a seller who breaches a contract by refusing to sell after the contract has been signed may be liable to a two-year statute of limitations for filing a case against them. Following that, the buyer has two years to file a lawsuit against the seller in federal court. If the buyer waits any longer than that, the contract becomes unenforceable, and any legal action will be fruitless in the long run. When evaluating whether or whether a contract is enforceable under the law of laches, the passage of time is also taken into account.

The concept of laches requires that a claim be brought as soon as possible after it has accrued an unreasonable amount of time. It is necessary to consider the idea of laches when there is no statute of limitations imposing a time restriction on taking action to protect one's rights. Generally speaking, estoppel is a legal rule of evidence that precludes a person from making an allegation or denial that contradicts what the person has previously claimed to be true in a court of law. A contract cannot say or commit to something and then later seek to take a position that is diametrically opposed to that expressed or committed in the contract. The individual's words or actions will "prevent" them from participating in such behavior. A contract made as a consequence of a factual error is void and unenforceable, and it cannot be enforced in any court of jurisdiction.

The objective of a legal contract, as previously indicated, must be permissible by the laws of the country in which it is entered into. It is not legitimate until this condition is met; else, the agreement is void. When someone enters into a contract to deceive the other party, the agreement is deemed illegitimate. For example, a homeowner may collaborate with an appraiser to inflate the value of their property to get a bigger mortgage from the lender. It is determined that the contract with the appraiser is null and void since both parties entered into it intending to cheat the other. The mortgage contract between the property owner and the bank is voidable in the previous case because the owner misrepresented information about the property throughout the loan application procedure (its value). When a victim, in this case, the bank, believes that they have been misrepresented, they may be able to have a contract cancelled.

On the other hand, misrepresentation is not legally binding on the other person in question. The omission to provide critical information and the use of undue influence over one or both parties are examples of similar behavior. Initial considerations are that the contract is legitimate and enforceable; nevertheless, if any one of the faults stated above is proven, the contract will be voidable and unenforceable as a result of that flaw.

Chapter 7: Types of Contracts

Contracts come in a variety of shapes and varieties. Each has its own set of rules for how it is entered into; in certain cases, they may even be similar to one another in some ways. For example, suppose both parties have exchanged obligations to do specific activities. In that case, an explicit contract may also be referred to as a bilateral contract or a bilateral agreement, depending on the context. As a listing agreement, an explicit contract in the form of a net listing, which must be in writing owing to the nature of the contract (it is a listing agreement), is also a bilateral contract in the sense that both the seller and the broker have agreed to specific performance. The seller has given their approval to enable the broker to sell the property, and the broker has agreed to accept a commission based on the difference between the selling price and the amount that the seller wishes to earn from the sale of the property. The parties to a transaction will completely and clearly specify and agree on the activities that will be done or not taken by each party under the terms of the contract in an express contract, also known as a written agreement. Express contracts may be written or oral contracts, and they can be official or informal, depending on the circumstances. In the case of an agency agreement, which allows a seller the exclusive right to sell and which is signed by both the seller and the broker, this is an example of an explicitly written contract.

Express contracts are the most prevalent kind of real estate transaction in which you will engage. Participants in an implied contract, which is always an oral contract, act as if they are parties to a formal written agreement, despite the fact that they are not. Whenever a homeowner decides to sell their house, they employ a real estate agent to assess the property and advise her on what they need to do to get the property ready for sale. In addition to painting and new carpets, the realtor makes additional recommendations and the owner follows through on those recommendations. The realtor then invites potential buyers to see the property in question. In spite of the fact that neither the seller nor the agent ever signs a contract, an implicit contract exists between them due to the seller's failure to object to the agent's actions during the transaction.

The question is, how much is the agent's commission in this particular instance? It is possible to enter into a unilateral contract where one party pledges to do something only if and when the other party agrees to do something else. The first person's commitment to act is conditional on the second person actually acting in response to their promise made in the first person's commitment to act. Individual contracts in the real estate sector include options to buy a house and open listing agreements, which are both instances of unilateral contracts in the industry. Example: In a contingent fee agreement, one party (the seller) promises to do something (such as pay a commission to a broker) if and only if the other party (the realtor) finds a willing and able buyer. The realtor may or may not be capable of finding a willing and able buyer, but has not made any promises to do so. A bilateral contract is one in which both parties agree to carry out a certain action in return for promises from the other. If a buyer commits to purchasing a property at the price that the seller and the buyer have agreed upon, the seller must agree to sell that property to the buyer at that price or risk losing their deposit.

A purchase agreement is what this is formally known as.

The buyer makes a payment to the seller in the agreed-upon amount, and the seller transfers ownership of the property to the buyer in exchange. The following contract has been completed: It is only after that all the terms and the conditions of the agreement have been satisfied that a contract may be considered fully executed. An example of a contract that has been fulfilled includes the buyer paying the seller the purchase money and the seller relinquishing possession of the goods purchased. An executory contract is a contract that is still in the process of being finished when the contract is executed. In this specific case, some of the sentences, or maybe all of them, have not yet been fully completed. At the end of the transaction, a buyer agency agreement serves as an executory contract that lasts until the buyer obtains ownership of the property that they wish to acquire. Conditions and contingencies may be added to a real estate sales contract by either the buyer or the seller, and these conditions and contingencies are referred to as "contingencies." Contingencies can be added to a real estate sales contract for a variety of reasons. The term "condition" refers to anything that one or both of the parties are required to do or accomplish, or it may refer to anything regarding the object that is being sold or acquired. In certain instances, it may be essential to include a condition in the sales contract stating that the appliances must be in good functioning order at the time of the closing. Depending on the circumstances, it is conceivable that a condition of sale may demand, for example, that the premises be turned over "empty of the seller's things and in broom clean condition."

The majority of the time, they are contractual obligations that must be met prior to the contract's expiry. If the seller fails to comply with the terms of the agreement, the transaction may be postponed until the seller complies with the terms of the agreement. Instead, in the event of an air conditioning system that is not operating properly and is not repaired in accordance with the contract, it is common for the parties to reach an agreement to subtract a set sum from the selling price as compensation.

Essentially, a contingency is a statement—a clause—that specifies a specific action that must be done before the contract can be declared valid. Contracts for residential transactions often contain contingencies such as the examination of a home, the purchase of a mortgage, and the selling of an existing property. Unsatisfactory performance of a contingency in a contract is often a significant provision that is so critical to a buyer's interests that the contract can/will be cancelled if the contingency does not meet its requirements.

The contingencies of a contract are often (but not always) met early in the contract's lifetime, allowing the deal to be completed on time. An inspection contingency may be one or more inspections that may be necessary, for example, which would be typical. A buyer will have "x" number of days after the signing of the contract to have the property inspected by a pest control inspector to determine whether or not there are any pest concerns. The seller is responsible for eradicating any pest problems that are detected and providing a certificate from a pest control professional within a certain length of time after the problem is discovered. The buyer may/will be allowed to cancel the contract without incurring any costs or penalties if the seller fails to do so within the specified time frame. The seller will be obligated to reimburse the deposit if the seller does not comply.

As an example, if it is found that a property is located in a flood zone, and the contract says that the sale is conditional on the property not being located in a flood zone, the transaction will almost always be cancelled. It is possible for the party that intends to benefit from a contract to waive a contract contingency (as well as a contract condition). It is also possible for a sales contract to have limits and inclusions that are particular to the product or service being sold. A seller may opt to exclude some items from the sale of her property, such as the dining room chandelier and the rosebush that Aunt Mildred gave her as a wedding gift. Occasionally, a buyer may request that a seller remove a refrigerator from the property, which is not generally considered a fixture in that area.

The vendor may accept this request. Both parties must agree on both exclusions and inclusions before signing the contract to guarantee that the items are included in the final sales contract when completed. Both the buyer and the seller affirm that they have read and understood the terms and conditions of the contract by signing it. This section discusses the facts and clauses that must and may be included in a real estate sales contract, also known as an agreement of sale or contract of sale, as well as the terms and conditions of the agreement. This part also discusses the terms and conditions of the agreement. On the other hand, a long and drawn-out procedure involving an offer and a counteroffer may be required to reach the acceptance/contract stage. Multiple more offers may be made in response to one from a buyer during this negotiation period.

A binding contract exists between the buyer and the seller until the seller makes a counteroffer. The offer has ceased to be legitimate, and the counteroffer has become legally binding on both the buyer and the seller. If a buyer rejects a seller's counteroffer, the counteroffer is deemed invalid. When an offer or counteroffer is accepted, it is deemed to be a binding contract, and the offertory is notified in writing of the decision. Before it, there is no agreement between the buyer and the seller on the purchase price. A typical procedure is for the offeree's agent to notify the offertory's agent, who then informs the offertory of the notice as soon as they receive it. Because there is no contract in place at any stage throughout this procedure, either the buyer or the seller has the option to walk away from a potential deal at any point during the process. Due to the lack of a binding contract, either the buyer or the seller may withdraw their offer or counteroffer at any moment without penalty.

This is a fundamental concept to keep in mind: neither party is obligated to participate in discussions with another. When a party makes an offer or counteroffer, the other party is often given a certain amount of time in which to respond with an acceptance or rejection of the offer or counter offer. During that period, which might last as short as 24 hours, the offertory has the right to withdraw the offer/counteroffer from the offeree at any time and without incurring any penalties. Once an offer or counteroffer has been accepted, the offertory is under no duty to keep the offer or counteroffer on the table indefinitely. The acceptance of the offer or counteroffer results in the formation of a contract; however, the formal sales contract may still need to be negotiated after that.

It is possible that certain elements, such as exclusions and inclusions, may need to be worked out before the agreement can be completed.

 It is customary in certain areas and markets to use a binder at this stage to keep everything together and organized. When a buyer and a seller sign the binder, they are agreeing to continue working toward a final sales contract. The binder contains the essential conditions of acceptance and "binds" the buyer and seller to continue working toward a final sales contract. In addition, as a demonstration of good faith, the buyer may make a "good faith" payment of $1,000 or more. Following the signing of the contract by both parties, there may be a three-day review period to allow both parties to evaluate the agreement. The legal counsel for each party carries out a review of the contract during this time, and at that point, any party (though often the buyer) has the right to reject the contract for any reason on the recommendation of their legal counsel.

As soon as the contract is approved, all good-faith money, along with the deposit balance, is sent to the seller's attorney, who will keep the monies in escrow until all of the necessary paperwork has been completed. If any revisions are required after the final sales contract has been signed, they may be made by adding riders to the contract. A rider is a kind of contract addendum that alters the contract conditions in which it is included. Riders are often added during the three-day review period of time before the event. All of the parties engaged in the transaction are signed and attested to by Riders. It is customary for the rider to include language that includes it into the contract as a whole at the opening of the document.

Even though the dining room chandelier is not being included in the transaction, a rider might stipulate that the chandelier will still be sold. After signing the final contract, the buyer is told to have earned equitable title to the property that they have just acquired. Although the legal title has been transferred, it will stay in the custody of the seller until the transaction is finalized. Because of the contract, if the property is damaged or destroyed, the buyer may be liable for financial loss as a result of the damage or destruction. There are rules in several jurisdictions that regulate whether a buyer or a seller is in danger of losing their deposit money, depending on the circumstances. For this reason, the sales contract should indicate which party will incur the loss and which party is responsible for paying the insurance premiums on the property until it is sold. On the other hand, an insurance company will claim that the buyer does not have an insurable interest in the property under consideration. As a consequence, in most cases, the seller is liable for the insurance.

Any party to the transaction has the right to walk away at any time until the offeree has accepted it and the offer or has been informed that the offer has been accepted. When there is no justifiable cause to withdraw from an accepted offer or counteroffer, the act of walking away from the negotiation has implications. Pretend you're in the following situation: Two hours before the closing, the buyer is completing the last walk-through and finds a large leak from a second-floor bathroom into the property's kitchen. In this case, the buyer finds that it would be excessively costly to remove asbestos from the pipes below the ceiling, and they notify the realtor that they will not be acquiring the home as a result. Is this an acceptable reason in this case? There are two options available to sellers: either they agree and both parties unilaterally rescind the contract, or they disagree and initiate a case against the buyer in small claims court. If one or both parties fail to fulfill their responsibilities under the contract of sale, they may be entitled to pursue one or more of the remedies listed below:

Cancellation of the contract

Consider the chance that the seller will not complete the transaction. This results in the seller canceling the contract and returning all of the buyer's money to him or her. This is a choice that has been taken without consulting anybody else.

Consider the following scenario: the seller chooses not to sell, and at the same time, the buyer obtains a better job offer in another location. A mutual, or bilateral, the decision is made by both parties; the seller then reimburses the buyer for the earnest money that was paid at the time of the agreement.

Cancellation of a contract: In the preceding scenario, the seller is still interested in selling, but the buyer has opted to take a job offer in a different place in lieu of completing the transaction. It is possible that the buyer may lose their entitlement to the contract and, more importantly, the earnest money. The following are the measures to take to make a claim for compensatory damages:

When one party is wounded under a contract, the other party has the option to launch a lawsuit against the injured party, asking to compensate the damages. Compensatory damages are monetary losses that the plaintiff claims to have incurred due to the defendant's violation of the contract in a breach of contract action. In this example, assume that the seller agrees to remove an in-ground pool at the buyer's request as a condition of the sale agreement with him. The consumer has now decided that they will not make a purchase. According to the seller, the pool removal was solely at the buyer's request, and as a result, the seller is entitled to reimbursement for reasonable replacement expenditures incurred in reinstalling the pool. Additional remedies include suing for lost profits while the transaction is still underway since the market has now collapsed, for attorney's fees, and keeping the deposit due to the buyer's failure to comply with the terms of the contract.

Specific performance lawsuit

The party that has been wronged brings a lawsuit against the other party to force the other party to comply with the terms of the agreement. If the seller has changed their mind, the buyer may take the seller to court to force the seller to sell, and vice versa if the seller has changed their mind, the buyer may take the seller to court to compel the seller to purchase.

On the other hand, a seller has the right to take a buyer to court to force him or her to finish the purchase transaction. On the other hand, specific performance may only be accessed when money is inadequate to provide the essential treatment.

According to this scenario, the family that is interested in acquiring the property may find themselves in this situation. A seller will often be forced to pay for monetary damages to avoid a lawsuit.

For the most part, everything you've just read has dealt with conventional real estate sales contracts, which are most often used in the context of residential properties. In order to pass the exam and maybe get a job in the industry of real estate, you must be acquainted with the many various types of real estate contracts that exist. A lease on a piece of rental property is one example of a kind of lease.

Land contracts, also known as installment sales contracts or installment contracts, and contract for deeds are all phrases that are used to describe the process of purchasing and selling property under the terms of an agreement known as a land contract. Typically, in this kind of real estate sales transaction, the vendee pays just a part of the purchase price upfront, with the remaining balance being paid in monthly installments or installments over many months or years. The vendee obtains equitable title in return for the down payment, but not full title due to the transaction. When purchasing real estate, the purchaser must either make a certain number of installment payments or pay the whole purchase price in one lump sum to ensure that the seller retains full title and ownership of the property.

The contract contains the terms and circumstances for making payments to the other party. While in most situations, the vendor keeps ownership of the property during this period, the vendee is not entitled to make any alterations to it unless the vendor gives their consent beforehand. The use of this kind of contract is required when obtaining finance for the buyer is a challenging task for the buyer. When a builder wants to finance the purchase of a large tract of land from a real estate developer for a subdivision but is unable to obtain a favorable interest rate on a business loan, he approaches the developer with a proposal to enter into a land contract with the developer, which the developer accepts.

On the other hand, if the builder fails to perform under the contract, for example, as a result of bankruptcy, it may be difficult for the owner to sell the property due to the previously established contract, which is detrimental to the developer. This is referred to as a "cloud on the title" in legalese since it is a cloud over the title.

In the case of purchasing an option, a person acquires the right to buy a property for the given amount within a certain time period. However, if the buyer chooses to acquire the property, the seller is compelled to sell it at the agreed-upon price. The buyer is under no obligation to purchase the property. In return for agreeing to the optioning, the seller receives a payment from the potential buyer. This money may or may not be used toward the property's purchase price, depending on the conditions of the option contract that both parties have agreed to.

Chapter 8: Describing Property & Appraising It

Legal descriptions are required for both real estate sales contracts and leasing agreements because they provide a thorough description of the property. A tenant must be informed of the kind of unit that is being leased as well as the area in which the unit is being rented. A buyer's right to be fully informed about the things he or she is purchasing is essential. Was the tree in the unfenced backyard behind the house included in their purchase, or was the tree on the next neighbor's land included in their acquisition? The tree and the additional 40 square feet in the backyard will not only raise the value of the property, but they will also increase the value of the land around the house.

However, although real estate appraisers are responsible for assessing the value of a property, they should be familiar with their work in order to do their own duties effectively and because they may be asked questions on their licensing exam about how property is valued. Additionally, the procedures of surveying and describing real estate may be characterized in the same way. While it is not necessary to be an expert in surveying in order to pass the exam, it is recommended that you be acquainted with the foundations of the different systems used. However, the boundary line that encircles the tree within the property in the preceding example would be included in the legal description of that property.

When it comes to a legal description of real estate, the only item that is given are the borders of the property. There are no mentions of any buildings or physical components such as a pond or trees in the story. The legal description of the property is included in the deed, and it specifies what is being acquired. The word "lawful" is crucial in the previous paragraph since it indicates that something is legal. To the extent permitted by law, it suggests that the description meets a number of specified requirements. Furthermore, the description must be prepared according to widely accepted legal standards, be legal enough to identify the property and establish that the property's identity is unique from that of any other real property in existence. If there was no legal description accessible, it would be far more difficult to buy and sell real estate. In most cases, one of the three processes indicated below is utilized to arrive at a legal description: metes and bounds, lot and block system, or rectangular survey system (see below for more information).

Every one of the three survey methods is in use in every part of the nation, however the rectangular survey system is used less commonly in the Northeast and Middle Atlantic states, as well as in North, South and Georgia, which were the first states to be colonized by English colonists. In the United States, all three systems are in operation at the moment. In certain areas, the metes and bounds technique is the most often used system, although the rectangular survey system is utilized in the majority of the rest of the country, including the rest of the United States. Contrary to this, the lot and block design is frequently used in subdivisions across the United States.

Furthermore, it may be used to create tax maps, which is a useful tool. From the northeast corner of Main Street and Oak Road, travel 300 feet east 9000'0" along Oak to a point; then north 9000'0" 300 feet to another point; then west 90 00'0" 300 feet to another point; and then south 9000'0" 300 feet along Main to the point and location of starting. a. A surveyor who uses the metes and bounds approach divides an area into the points of a compass and then goes clockwise around a circle, giving both direction information (compass points) as well as measurement information (measurements are provided by the surveyor) (distance). It's also worth noting that the description begins with the phrase "point of starting." This is quite crucial. Additionally, this is the point to which the boundary line must return in order for it to be considered a major reference point. Metes and bounds are a kind of system that is similar to the monument system in that it divides land into squares. Instead of utilizing lengths and directions to define borders, the monument system uses identifiers to describe them. These are monuments or landmarks that function as landmarks and act as reference points for the monument system. Naturally occurring or artificially produced, which indicates that they were made by humans. Beginning at the intersection of Main Street and Oak Street, and continuing down Oak Street to the creek bed, and then continuing down the creek bed to the fence, and then returning to the starting point, what happens if the stream is diverted or vanishes entirely, or if the neighbor chooses to demolish the barrier and start over? One of the disadvantages of a description based only on monuments is that it is limited in scope.

They have the capacity to change or be removed from a situation. Depending on who is doing the referencing, the lot and block system may also be referred to as the documented plat—not plot—system, the recorded map system, or the lot block tract system. In a development, a plat is a map that depicts the positions of the properties inside the development. Each block of the development has a number of lots, and each lot is split into a number of other lots. In addition to a lot number and a block number, each lot is designated by the following: Block 10, Lot 56. Along with roads and physical features like lakes, the map depicts a number of different locations. The surveyor uses the metes and bounds method in order to produce a description of the parcels of land under consideration. If this were not done, no one would be able to determine where Lot 56 ends and the surrounding lots begin.

What Is the Purpose of a Real Estate Appraisal?

The purpose of a real estate appraisal is to ascertain the approximate market value of a piece of real estate before it is purchased. Owners may need an assessment of the current value of their property in order to refinance their mortgage or determine a fair selling price for it on the open market. When a potential buyer wants to get a mortgage, he or she has to have an appraisal done first. Several additional justifications for having a property appraised have something to do with government procedures in one way or another. In order for the government to be able to take property via the exercise of its right of eminent domain, the property must first be appraised in order to ascertain its fair market value in the eyes of the property's original owner.

The value of a property must also be determined in order to determine the payment of estate taxes in the event of a person's death, or the payment of gift taxes when a person gives or receives real property as a gift. It also assists in the construction of a tax basis, which allows for the computation of any gains or losses that may result from the sale of the property in the future. Worth is defined as the monetary equivalent of an item's relative value, expressed in terms of money, expressed in terms of another object. A dollar and cent value are a monetary value in the real estate market that refers to how much money buyers and sellers believe a piece of property is worth in terms of dollars and cents.

When it comes to determining the value of real estate or any other commodity, there are four elements to consider. The ability to fulfil a buyer's desire or demand is referred to as the utility of a product or service. a lack of available resources the ability to transport information (ability to convey title by selling, leasing, bequeathing, or giving away the property) Make a compelling case for your position (ability to pay for what is wanted or needed) In order to be valued, a property must have all four of the characteristics stated above. There are, however, various different forms of value to take into consideration. There are many types of value in real estate that must be understood before investing in real estate:

The current market value

According to the definition provided by the Code of Federal Regulations, market value is "the most reasonable price that a property might fetch in a competitive and open market given all of the conditions essential for a fair sale." The terms "market value" and "price" are not synonymous. The final price of a property (i.e., the total of what a buyer is prepared to pay and what a seller is willing to accept) may be more or lower than the market worth of the property. The value of a company's stock fluctuates during the course of its existence. A real estate appraiser is a professional who determines the market value of a piece of real estate in question. It is possible to determine the value of an item by contemplating how it will be used or what it will accomplish in a certain context. "Value in use" is the term used to describe this.

For example, a restaurant has monetary value just by virtue of the fact that it is a restaurant. The restaurant would be of less value to someone trying to acquire property and create a retail store due to the amount of renovation necessary, but it would be fairly useful to someone looking to establish a restaurant business because of the amount of remodeling required.

Investment value, as opposed to market value, is the value of a property to someone (an investor) who plans to use it for a specific purpose and does not consider the property's current market value.

Because the restaurant property in the preceding example is suited for the restaurateur's needs, he or she may be willing to spend a specific amount on the purchase of the property. Someone wishing to start a company selling men's garments in the area, on the other hand, may discover opportunities in the building if it were completely reconstructed. Thus, the potential shop owner would understand that the property is valuable as an investment, but he or she would be willing to pay less (than the restaurant owner) for it.

Estimated monetary value: The assessed value of a piece of property is the amount of money that a government official known as a tax assessor assigns to the asset in question. Real estate taxes are computed on the basis of the assessed value of the property, which is decided by the county assessor. Ad valorem taxation is used to determine the amount of tax due, which implies that it is computed in proportion to the value of the item subject to tax. Even though it may seem trite, acquiring a home is frequently the most expensive decision that an individual or couple will make in their life. When it comes to deciding whether or not to acquire a home, some economic concepts influence people's choices whether or not they are conscious of it.

This is also true for people who are interested in owning commercial real estate or leasing office space for their company. When appraising real estate, appraisers should be familiar with the following economic ideas, which have an influence on the value of the property: Both supply and demand are two sides of the same coin, as the saying goes. Both supply and demand are essential economic principles, and they are intertwined. As the supply of a product grows, the demand for that commodity decreases. The lower the demand is while the supply is increasing or remaining constant, the less expensive something will be in the long term, and vice versa. The stronger the demand for something while the supply of that item drops or remains constant, the higher the price of that item will be in the market. This holds true in the real estate sector as well as in other industries. Due to a lack of buyers, a housing surplus reduces house prices (value decreases); while, a scarcity of houses in a desirable area enables a seller to ask for a higher selling price (value rises—if the buyer can find a seller willing to pay) and therefore increases the worth of the property.

Competition: It is true that sellers must compete to attract buyers when the market is a "buyers' market," but in a "sellers' market," buyers must compete in order to acquire the property they genuinely desire. The difference between a buyers' market and a sellers' market is that buyers' markets have an excess of available homes, while sellers' markets have a shortage of available properties. As a consequence of the competition, the imbalance between supply and demand is restored to its original state. While competitive forces may push the market to one extreme or the other, they can also push the market to the other extreme, from a shortage of available properties that pushes up prices to a scarcity of buyers that drives down prices, among other things. For the purpose of fulfilling their wishes and needs, consumers, including renters, will look for the least expensive choice that will suit all of their specifications and criteria. The most crucial thing to remember is that equal value is critical in this situation.

It is necessary for the appraiser to first discover what the market considers "equal" in order to ascertain what the market considers "comparable." Supply and demand are always changing, and as such, while assessing the value of real estate, it is necessary to take this into consideration as well. Buying a comparable home and selling it for $300,000 a month later does not always mean that the same house will sell for $300,000 in the near future. Depending on the conditions, it might be more or less than that. For example, the housing crisis that preceded the recession that began in 2007 gave a clear representation of this concept, with property values in certain parts of the country decreasing on a weekly basis in some areas.

Purchasing with the expectation of capital appreciation (sometimes known as "buying for appreciation"): For many years, homeowners made their purchases with the belief that their investment would grow in value as they took use of the numerous benefits of living in their newly purchased home. These are the benefits that people expect to get when they acquire a piece of real estate, and they are based on the dual expectations of gain and use (utility). Depending on how they interact, these market factors may either boost or diminish the value of a piece of real estate. The predicted closure of a neighboring industry, which would result in a drop-in economic activity in the surrounding region, will have an impact on real estate prices in the area.

A boost in property values will result from the expectation of a firm constructing a facility, as well as the resulting increase in economic activity. If we use the term proportionality in this situation, we are referring to the condition of being in balance. Remember from your economics classes that there are four components of production: land, labor, capital, and entrepreneurship. These four components are as follows: Attained when all of the components are in balance, or in proportion to one another, is the maximum value. Pretend you're in the following situation:

A neighborhood consists of residences that are all valued at between $200,000 and $300,000 per house. In one instance, a buyer purchases one of these homes, demolishes it, and then builds a $850,000 McMansion on the site of the demolished house. In this case, the land has been overdeveloped, and a disproportionate number of resources have been spent in comparison to the relative value of the property in the region. Because of the McMansion, the delicate balance of values in the surrounding neighborhood has been disrupted. Productivity that is superior than the norm: The value of developed land is determined by the amount of excess output it generates. Calculate the amount of surplus productivity that has been created by subtracting the cost of the inputs into the production process from the total net revenue. Consider the following scenario: a developer builds a strip mall and rents out all of the stores in it to different tenants. Year after year, the assets create $1.2 million in rental revenue for the owner, while the expenditures of administering the mall total $750,000, resulting in a surplus productivity of $450,000 every year. Adding Value: According to this idea, the worth of something is not assessed in terms of its cost, but rather in terms of the value that it adds to or subtracts from the overall value of the property.

When estimating the value of real estate via the use of the sales comparison approach, this is an important factor to consider. When establishing the value of a condo, an appraiser must consider factors such as how much a Parkside view boosts the value of one unit and how much a view of an air shaft diminishes the value of another flat, all other things being equal.

Income that is rising and decreasing (diminishing) in value: A property's worth will increase by a higher amount than the cost of any additional features that are added to the property, up to a point. However, there comes a point at which additional features are no longer worth the money they take to implement. Known as the point of diminishing returns, this is the point at which the rate of return begins to decline.

Pretend you're in the following situation: A seller prepares a house for sale by constructing a half bath on the first floor, when none previously existed, in order to attract buyers. In return for an additional $2,000 in profit, the seller incurs costs of $6,500 but obtains sales revenues of $8,500, resulting in a net profit of $2,000 for the seller. Meanwhile, the vendor will repaint the inside and replace the carpet as part of his services. However, even if it costs the seller $5,000, it only adds $4,000 to the ultimate sales price of the house. As a result, the seller gets a refund of $1,000, which is $1,000 less than the cost.

The most important and most advantageous application: The most profitable and legally permissible use of a property is the most profitable and legally permissible use that may be made of the asset. Establish what the highest and best use of the property is in order to determine its market worth at the beginning of the process. If a site's use is legal and lawful, the word "legally lawful" relates to whether the use planned for the property is permissible under local zoning restrictions. In addition to whether or not it is legally permissible, there are three more variables that are taken into account when evaluating the highest and best use: whether or not it is physically feasible, whether or not it is financially feasible, and whether or not it is maximally productive.

The first three decide which business will be the most productive, and hence the most profitable, for the property, and which business will be the most profitable for the property. When an appraisal is performed on improved land rather than unoccupied property, the appraiser considers the viability of the buildings on the land in relation to the highest and best use for which the land is most suitable at the time of the appraisal. This is known as the highest and best use test. A proposal to destroy them, rehabilitate them in some way, or leave them in their existing state may be put up by the appraiser. For example, demolition might be carried out on an abandoned gas station on a piece of land that was to be developed into a shopping mall.

Conformity, progression, and regression are all terms that are used in the field of psychology to describe various phenomena. Conformity is enforced in a subdivision by the use of restrictive covenants and homeowner association laws, which may include limits on the color of front door paint. However, even if an owner may not enjoy the uniformity, it helps reduce one potential challenge when valuing real estate: determining how the prices of your neighbors' properties affect the worth of your own. The purpose of zoning regulations in towns and cities is to maintain a certain level of consistency by limiting the size of lots and the basic architectural style, but people are still allowed to express their uniqueness and creativity in the buildings they build within those boundaries. While it is possible that a nonconforming house, such as a mid-century modern in a neighborhood of colonials, would have a lower value, this is not necessarily the true in real estate. When the houses in a community are similar (conform), they contribute to the overall value of the area by increasing its appeal. There may be a similarity in terms of usage (for example, all single-family houses or all semi-detached homes), or in terms of architectural design (for example, all ranch-style homes) (for example, all mid-century modern or all colonial). The concepts of development and regression are intimately linked to the idea of compliance in a number of ways. If the price of a stock is growing, this is referred to as progression; if the price is decreasing, this is referred to as regression.

It's similar to the notion of guilt by association in certain ways. When the value of mid-century modern homes in a neighborhood of small colonials rises as a consequence of increased buyer interest in the area as a whole, the value of the tiny colonials will rise as well. An expensive McMansion situated in the Centre of Cape Cod would lose value over time as people's interest in the region waned. One must take into account social factors such as celebrity status and leisure activities. Other factors to consider include family orientation and homeowner limits. It is a measure of how desirable it is to reside in some locations as opposed to others in terms of status. The closeness of a property to certain types of recreational or cultural activities, such as tennis courts and museums, as well as other factors, may have an impact on the value of the property. When describing a place, the term "family orientation" is used to describe how family-friendly it is to be there. What is the district's performance on state-mandated assessments like the ACT? What is the percentage of students who graduate from high school? Is there any space available for sponsored sports teams to practice on sports fields? Is there a pool of after-school programmers to choose from?

Typically, these four factors would be considered to increase the value of a property in general, even if a particular buyer is disinterested in any or all of them in a particular case. A homeowner's association's restrictive covenants may boost or reduce the value of a property depending on the nature of the covenants and how a buyer feels about being limited in how he or she uses the property, among other factors. All of the economic factors that affect the value of a piece of real estate property include the local economy, interest rates, vacancies, rentals, parking, corner influence, and plottage, to name a few. It's important to keep track of how many of these factors are impacted by the rules of supply and demand. If the local economy is experiencing difficulties, it is probable that the residential and commercial real estate markets will be experiencing difficulties as well.

Foreclosures, defaults on rent and mortgage payments, as well as a glut of property on the market, will all result from a recession in the local economy, which will result in a reduction in property values as a result of the contraction. Aside from that, interest rates have an influence on the value of the asset. If interest rates remain high, the building of new houses will be hindered because borrowing money to finance construction projects would become prohibitively costly. Additionally, it means that mortgage rates will rise as a consequence of this decision. While fewer new homes mean that older properties become more desirable to buyers, high mortgage rates also mean that fewer buyers are prepared to make the investment necessary to acquire a home. People are more likely to be interested in owning a home when borrowing rates are low, on the other hand, when borrowing rates are high.

The rate of vacancy in a building may also be affected by interest rates. At a period when interest rates are cheap, it is feasible that developers would build more houses in a particular place than there are tenants available. As a result, there is an excessive amount of inventory on the market, as well as a high percentage of vacancy in the rental market. It is possible that this situation will have an impact on commercial and industrial buildings in addition to residential ones.

It is possible that the value of a commercial property will be lower if the vacancy rate is taken into consideration during the appraisal of the structure than if the vacancy rate were lower in the structure. Rental rates that are too high lead to a rise in the number of individuals who want to own property, while low rental rates lead to a drop in the number of people who want to become property owners. It is more likely that the former will lead to an increase in value, whilst the latter will lead to a decrease in value. When it comes to property value, the existence of parking and the placement of that parking are important considerations. According to the National Association of Realtors, a townhouse with a garage is worth much more money than a townhouse without a garage.

The assessment of a townhouse that is an end unit, or corner apartment, will be higher than the assessment of a townhouse that is an interior unit, assuming all other elements are equal. For example, a free-standing property at the intersection of two streets would be worth less than a house in the Centre of the block because of the increased traffic, noise, and loss of privacy. It is the process of grouping several properties to generate a total value that exceeds the sum of the values of the individual parcels, which is known as plottage. Property value is affected by a variety of political issues that are straightforward to understand: taxes, zoning regulations, rent control, growth restrictions, environmental regulations, and construction and health regulations, among others. Taxes are one of the most obvious political issues that influence property value. By imposing restrictions, which are often monetary in nature, this collection of traits may have a negative influence on value, either directly (via taxes) or indirectly (through regulation), which may have a negative impact on value (through compliance). However, they have the potential to have a positive influence on the value of a property. Low taxes may result in increased demand for real estate and, as a consequence, higher assessments of real estate.

A property zoned for commercial use will produce more tax revenue than a property zoned for residential use, and its value will be higher than a property zoned for residential use. A property zoned for commercial use will create more tax revenue than a property zoned for residential use. Apart from that, the taxes collected via commercial zoning may be used to balance residential taxes, resulting in lower property taxes for residential property owners, which in turn raises the value of their homes.

As a consequence of smart growth limitations, there may be an increase in demand for homes and rental properties, which may lead to a rise in property prices. Location! This may be the most important factor to consider when purchasing or renting a property. Whether a property is in close vicinity to what a person wishes, such as recreational places, museums, public transportation, and so on. Environmental factors such as climate, water supply, particularly for commercial and industrial enterprises, transportation network, view, size and shape of the property (for example, a regularly shaped parcel versus a pie-shaped parcel), exposure (i.e., in which direction the sun rises and sets), environmental hazards, and the physical layout of the land are all taken into consideration (for example, a stream running through a suburban property would add value, whereas a rood running through a rural property would detract value). The three ways that appraisers employ to assess the value of a piece of property are the sales comparison technique, the cost approach, and the income strategy. The sales comparison technique is the most often used methodology. When it comes to single-family homes, the sales comparison method is the one that is most often used. It is used to examine the subject property (the property that is being appraised), and it compares it to similar properties that have sold in the past or are currently on the market in order to determine its value. It is referred to as the market comparison technique in certain circles. While the costs of each component's components as well as the expenses of installation are listed separately in the unit-in-place approach, the costs of the unit-out-of-place methodology are grouped together.

The indexing method is as follows: However, although the index methodology is the least accurate of the four methods, it is useful as a quick approach to estimating spending in today's dollars if the original building prices are known, and if the original construction costs are known, and if the original building prices are known.

To measure the relative change in building costs over time, construction cost indices, similar to the consumer price index, which tracks the relative change in prices for particular consumer products over time, are available to track the relative change in construction costs over time. Consumer price indexes (CPIs) are used to measure the relative change in prices for certain consumer items over the course of time. Consider the situation of a ranch house built in 1954 at a cost of $30,000 to $40,000 to build. When the construction cost index for that kind of home was computed in 1954, it was 80; now, it is 180 for the same style of home, according to the index. After the appraiser has determined the cost of the modifications, he or she must determine the amount of depreciation that should be applied to those upgrades. The difference between the initial worth of the improvements on the property and their current value would be represented by depreciation if the upgrades were brand new.

A variety of factors have contributed to the decline in the value of the improvements (structures) on the property. Wear and strain on the structure causes physical degradation, which may be either treatable or irreversible depending on the degree of the damage. The term "incurable" refers to a physical degradation that would cost more to cure than it would add to the value of the structure. Replacing water-damaged hardwood flooring would be a curable deterioration since the value that it would provide to the overall worth would outweigh the cost of installing new hardwood flooring in the first place, making it a worthwhile investment. It is a design flaw that may be either curable or irreversible, depending on the cost of fixing the defect vs the amount of value that will be added as a consequence of the remedy.

External obsolescence: Previously, the neighborhood was close to stores, an elementary school and restaurants; however, due to the construction of a shopping mall on the outskirts of town, most of the shops and restaurants have closed, and the elementary school has been relocated.

Internal obsolescence: Once upon a time, the neighborhood was close to stores, an elementary school and restaurants; however, due to the relocation of the elementary school, the neighborhood has become isolated. This is an example of the principle of external obsolescence in action. Despite the fact that the houses are still in decent shape, the surrounding neighborhood has changed significantly over the years. Outside of the manufacturing industry, external obsolescence is considered an unsolvable challenge.

As soon as the appraiser has identified which kind of depreciation will be employed, he or she must determine what depreciation factor will be used. For instance, the economic age-life methodology, sometimes known as the straight-line method, is an example of a standard strategy to estimating life expectancy. This technique is predicated on the assumption that an improvement loses value throughout the length of its economic life at a constant rate, and that the improvement's economic life ends when it no longer has the highest value for the property at which it was put at the outset of the operation. According to the definition, the economic life of an improvement is the amount of time that it contributes to the total value of the property during which it is in use.

Investment properties are valued using the income method, also known as the income capitalization approach, which measures the amount of money generated by a property and evaluates its worth based on that amount of revenue. While the estimate considers not just the current income (value), it also takes into consideration the future benefit (value) that the investor can expect to get in exchange for their investment. In order to compute this amount, first determine net operating income, and then calculate the rate of capitalization, which is a time-consuming and sophisticated procedure.

The first step taken by an appraiser is to estimate net operating income (NOI), which is achieved in four steps by the appraiser. An appraiser compiles information about a property's income and expenses from a range of sources, including the current owner's accounting firm and the property management business, and then compiles the information into a single report.

In the second phase, after acquiring all of the relevant information, the appraiser determines the potential gross income for the property (PGI). Taking into consideration that there are no vacancies on the property, this is the maximum amount of money that might be made. In order to compute the amount owing, the market rent (rather than contract rent) is utilized, rather than the actual rents paid. The rent that may be charged if market conditions were to prevail is referred to as the market rent. Property owners may make money from a number of ways other than rent. For example, charging for parking in an underground parking garage or a parking lot connected to the building might provide revenue for the property. Additionally, this income is taken into account while calculating PGI.

Third, the appraiser deducts from the PGI an allowance for vacancies as well as an allowance for nonpayment of rents or a loss on bad debt collection, if any, as well as any other appropriate adjustments. The net effective income is represented by the new number (EGI). Fourth, the EGI is lowered by the amount of the property's operating costs (including both fixed and variable expenses), as well as any reserves for replacement that have been established. It is important to differentiate between expenditures that are constant, such as property taxes, and those that are changeable, such as leasing commissions. Certain components, such as carpeting and paint, will need to be replaced over time, and the cost of these repairs will be accounted for in the reserve account for the building. When determining the value of a property, appraisers use all three methods of determining its worth: sales comparison, cost, and income.

Those of you who have studied the part above on how to become an appraiser will remember that the reconciliation procedure is the last step before creating the actual assessment report. After examining the results of the different methodologies, the appraiser comes up with a single value or range of values that is the most strongly supported by the information that has been acquired and analyzed in this stage. As the appraiser proceeds through the process, he or she will give more weight to some data points than to others, based on factors such as the amount of data points, the accuracy, the relevancy, and the reliability of the findings, among other things. Reconciliation is also a phrase that is used to describe the final conclusion that the appraiser makes about the value of a piece of real estate.

Chapter 9: Understanding Forms of Real Estate Ownership

There are many various forms of real estate ownership available to choose from. Owning real estate on your own is a viable possibility. The property may be owned jointly by you and your spouse. It is possible to co-own the property with other people. The possibility of becoming a stakeholder in a firm that owns real estate does exist. Purchases of real estate in the form of a condominium or cooperative association may also be possible. Individuals' concerns about ownership and the formalities that apply in each of these situations are substantially different.

In most cases, attorneys are in charge of identifying who has legal ownership of a piece of real estate in question. When you work as a real estate agent in some locations, especially those where attorneys play a lesser role in real estate transactions, you may find yourself dealing with these problems more directly than you would in other places.

Whatever level of involvement you have with various forms of ownership issues in a real estate transaction, state examiners want you to be aware of the various types of ownership. As I discuss various types of real estate ownership in this chapter, I will cover each type's fundamental vocabulary and significant characteristics, including owning property by yourself, owning a property with others, owning a property with your spouse, owning property in trust, and owning property through a corporation. I also look at specific types of ownership, such as cooperatives and condominiums, in addition to the traditional ones.

Although real estate agents manage the bulk of the responsibilities associated with acquiring and selling property in their jurisdictions, they nevertheless need to be continually aware of the components of the transaction with which they are not acquainted daily.

The ability to refer clients and consumers to real estate attorneys who are competent in real estate problems is essential when ownership difficulties become even the tiniest bit troublesome in terms of formality. Since real estate law has evolved to deal with these various forms of ownership, it has had to deal with them using different terminology and, in some cases, imposing entirely different conditions on each of them.

The fact that real estate can be owned by one person, two or more people (including a married couple), or a business is self-evident.

Pay special attention to the terminology used in this section and the underlying contrasts between the various types of property ownership. Identifying these differences will very definitely be the focus of exam questions on this subject matter. "Tenancy" is a phrase that will be used often throughout this section. The word "tenancy" refers to a legal right to use a piece of real estate for a certain purpose.

Although most of us associate the phrase with being a renter, which is basically correct, the term may also refer to having a financial interest in a piece of real estate. Be aware that the phrase will be used in both of its connotations in a state exam, so be prepared to see it. One last point to mention is that the term "tenancy" comes from a Latin word that literally translates to "to hold."

Sole ownership, also known as a tenancy in severalty, refers to the act of holding title to real property solely for one's personal benefit. I'm well aware that the law has done it yet another time. You're probably asking yourself right now, "

How can you use the word "severalty" when you're talking about a single individual?" In this particular instance, the approach is rather sensible. Rather than being derived from the word "several," the term "severalty" is derived from the word "sever," which literally means "cut off." When a person has exclusive ownership of a piece of property, all other interests in the property are terminated. Or, to put it another way, no one else has an ownership interest in the property other than the person who now owns it.

Concurrent ownership, often referred to as co-ownership, is a kind of property ownership that permits two or more people who are not married to own property in a joint venture. Co-ownership may be broken down into two types: tenancy in common and joint tenancy, both of which I will describe. In spite of the fact that these two similar types of ownership are available to married couples, it does not rule out that they will serve different purposes of ownership for persons who are not married as well. Finally, and perhaps most critically, one of the most fundamental differences between a joint tenant and a tenant in common is the right of survivorship you have as a joint tenant instead of the right you do not have as a tenant in common. A joint tenancy with the right of survivorship means that if one of the joint tenants dies, the other tenant(s) immediately become the legal owner of the deceased tenant's share of the real estate. This is known as the right of survivorship. Married couples who own real estate may elect to use joint tenancy as a kind of ownership arrangement. When one spouse dies, the other spouse immediately succeeds in the title of the sole owner of the property. For the benefit of a third party, it is conceivable for real estate to be owned by and held in trust for that third party.

Among the most important actors in a trust are:

- The trustor (the person who owns the property and transfers it to a trustee).
- The trustee (the person who receives the property and administers it on the beneficiary's behalf).
- The beneficiary (the person who receives the benefits of the property, like rent on an apartment house, as a result of the administration of the property by the trustee).

As an example, imagine you leave your apartment complexes to your brother in trust for your favorite nephew, and he comes to inherit them from you after you have passed away. Because you are the one who formed the trust, you are referred to as the trustor. While serving as trustee, your brother is in charge of the day-to-day management of all of your family's real estate holdings in line with the trust's provisions, which often allow for the transfer of income from the properties to your nephew. You have chosen your nephew as the receiver.

Suppose you are talking about corporate organizations that hold real estate. In that case, it is less about the ownership arrangements of the companies and more about the organizational structures of the companies themselves. Except if you have a significant amount of experience working with commercial real estate and developers, you are unlikely to be involved in this kind of transaction on a frequent basis in your normal real estate operations. According to the State Exam Authors, however, you will have some understanding of numerous commercial companies when you take the state test. If you are involved in a business venture, you may often hear the phrase "syndicate".

A syndicate does not constitute a form of ownership in the term's ordinary meaning. The term "real estate investment trust" refers to a group of people or corporations who get together to cooperate on a project or form a long-term partnership to own and manage buildings or other forms of real estate.

When it comes to real estate ownership, a corporation is treated in the same manner as an individual owner when it comes to the legal ramifications of the transaction. Suppose a corporation does not participate in co-ownership agreements with other firms. In that case, it is considered to hold property in the form of single ownership or tenancy in severalty, according to general principles of ownership. A corporation's real estate assets should have the following qualities, which are some of the most important: Despite the fact that individual shareholders own shares in a corporation, they do not have direct ownership rights in the company's assets, which may include real estate. In the case of a corporation's assets, shareholders have neither the authority nor the responsibility for their management. In most situations, a shareholder's liability is limited to the amount of money that the shareholder has invested in the company's stock.

Regardless of whether or not the corporation has the money, a shareholder who owns $1,000 worth of shares in a real estate investment corporation and the firm loses a lawsuit for millions of dollars can only lose his $1,000 investment and not anything more than the amount of money he has invested in the company. It is important to remember that a court of competent jurisdiction may overturn this protection in the event of litigation. When the corporation receives profits from the property, it is obligated to pay taxes on those earnings before distributing those profits to shareholders, who are then required to pay further taxes on the amounts received. In the United States, an S Company is a corporation with lower tax obligations and is permitted by the federal government under strict rules and regulations.

When two or more people or firms get together to do business, this is referred to as a partnership. In order to complete a single project, such as acquiring, refurbishing, and selling a building, or for a longer period of time, such as continuing investment and management of real estate assets, it is feasible to create a partnership with another party. As a result of the Uniform Partnership Act and the Uniform Limited Partnership Act, which have been passed in many states, real estate may be owned in either general or limited partnerships, depending on the circumstances.

Partnerships may be divided into two types: general partnerships and restricted partnerships. General partnerships are defined as those in which all of the partners have equal responsibility for the management and operational decisions that influence the functioning of the partnership. The partners are also personally accountable for any and all actions conducted by the partnership, without regard to the nature of the actions. By paying their taxes in line with their unique interests and responsibilities, the diverse partners are able to avoid paying double taxes. With limited partnerships, on the other hand, one general partner is often in control of the company's day-to-day operations, with many other limited partners having no such duty. Limited partnerships are also known as limited liability companies.

The limited partners' obligations are clearly defined and limited to the quantities of their respective interests in the company. As a hybrid organizational form in business, a limited liability corporation (LLC), often known as an LLC or a limited liability company (LLC), combines aspects of a partnership with those of a corporate structure. It is comparable to the liability of shareholders in that individual members of a corporation have a limited level of accountability for the organization's actions. Meanwhile, they are taxed as if they were partners in a general partnership, which is how they are treated. It is also conceivable for members of an LLC to run the firm in a more direct way than is allowed under a traditional general partnership structure.

The term "joint venture" refers to a situation in which two or more persons or firms get together to work on a single project, such as acquiring a home and renovating it before reselling it. A joint venture can possess property in a number of ways, such as a tenancy in common or joint tenancy or as a corporation, among other arrangements. However, due to the fact that joint ventures are not meant to be long-term economic relationships, the ownership agreement will nearly always include an end date. An acronym for a group of two or more persons or firms that come together to complete a real estate transaction is referred to as a joint venture, which is related to the term "syndicate." Another distinction between a joint venture and a syndicate is that a joint venture brings people together to work on a single real estate investment or project, whereas a syndicate typically works on a number of real estate investments or projects at the same time or a series of individual projects over an extended period of time, according to the definition. When it comes to condominium ownership, it is a kind of group ownership in which you are needed to get a deed to represent your individual ownership interest in the building. As a result of your tenant in common agreement, your deed explains your ownership interest in the airspace you own (also known as the unit) as well as your portion of the ground underneath and around the unit that you own. Each month, a homeowners association collects a certain amount of money from its members, which is used to pay for the maintenance of the condominium building and surrounding complex. Individual condominium owners are solely responsible for paying the required monthly contributions.

Chapter 10: Mortgages

A mortgage is a guarantee that a loan taken for the purpose of buying real estate will be repaid in full. However, even though the loan is granted by the lender (mortgagee), it is secured by the property that the borrower has provided as collateral (mortgagor). In states that function under the lien principle, a mortgage creates a lien against the title to the property that is the subject of the loan. When the mortgage is completely paid off, the lien on the property is removed. As long as the mortgage is in place, the mortgagor maintains both equitable and legal ownership of the property. A state that uses the title theory transfers only the legal title to the mortgagee, not the equitable title, as long as the state follows the rules. Upon complete repayment of the mortgage, the mortgagee becomes the legal owner of the property in issue, replacing the previous owner.

A note or promissory note that is associated with a piece of real estate, rather than a promise to repay a debt secured by it, explains how much money is owed, how and when it will be repaid, as well as the terms and situations under which it will not be repaid.

When a government-sponsored corporation, such as Freddie Mac, provides financing for real estate purchases, the use of a trust deed rather than a mortgage is authorized in certain jurisdictions.

A promissory note is required for the execution of a trust deed, just as it is for the execution of a mortgage. A trust deed is a legal document that transfers ownership of property from the trustor to a trustee acting on the beneficiary's behalf. According to the definition above, the trustor is the lender, the beneficiary is the one who began the financing, and the trustee is a third party in the transaction. In exchange for the trustor repaying the debt, a release deed is executed by the trustee, who then transfers the title of the property to the trustor. Because of assignments and assumptions, neither the original mortgagee nor the mortgagor may be involved in the mortgage repayment process by the time the mortgage is paid off. Both of these fees are often paid by a home loan or mortgage.

During an assignment, a new lender acquires a mortgage from the prior lender, or, in the case of a bank merger, accepts responsibility for the mortgage on behalf of the new lender. The ability of the lender to assign the mortgage is a fundamental element of the majority of mortgages in existence. Generally speaking, assumption refers to the procedure through which another party takes over ownership of a mortgage from the original mortgagor.

For example, a mother may sell her house to her son, who will then be responsible for paying the mortgage on the property in the future. Perhaps the son will assume responsibility for the mortgage and be held liable for the whole amount that has not been paid on the property. If he fails to make his mortgage payments on time, his mother will not be held accountable for the debt. On the other hand, the lender must provide their approval. (If the lender does not agree, the mother will be obliged to pay off her mortgage with the proceeds of the sale, and the son will be needed to get a mortgage of his own on the property.)

On the other hand, a purchaser may be required to take a mortgage under the conditions of a "subject to the mortgage" provision. A default on the mortgage by the purchaser to whom the mortgage was transferred will result in total liability for the original purchaser, who will be responsible for the whole amount.

Pretend you're in the following situation: This clause allows the mother (while she is still alive) to sell the house to her son, who subsequently takes the mortgage under the terms of the agreement. The son's mother is still accountable for the remaining amount of the mortgage if he fails to make his mortgage payments. Mortgagee permission is required in all cases before a mortgage may be transferred from one person to another. This is true regardless of the assumption.

Choosing between two "markets" when it comes to financing real estate is a difficult task. The primary and secondary mortgage markets are the two options available. Unlike stocks, mortgages originated (authored) in the primary market, and they are acquired (bundled) and sold as investments in the secondary market after they have been purchased (bundled). They are referred to as mortgage-backed securities (MBS), and securitization is the method through which they are created and packaged together. Because it produces income, it enables the primary market to continue to provide mortgages to customers. When interest rates on riskier mortgages began to climb and homeowners began to default on their loans, the housing market became the heart of the financial crisis that caused the recession that lasted from 2007 to 2009, the housing market was at the epicenter of the financial crisis. Because of waves of defaults that harmed the mortgages that served as the basis for the securitized mortgages, the issue swiftly spread to the secondary mortgage market, where it remains today.

Mortgages Markets

Mortgages are provided directly to potential buyers of residential property by the majority of the financial institutions in the first five kinds of financial organizations outlined above, to persons interested in purchasing a home or a condominium. Lenders specializing in portfolio lending offer financing for large-scale projects such as retail malls and housing developments. However, don't be fooled by the term "primary mortgage market," since mortgage brokers are not included in the main mortgage market. On the other hand, loan originators are responsible for finding the most beneficial interest rate and terms for borrowers; they do not originate loans for their own accounts. Particularly in the case of commercial real estate transactions, they serve as a conduit between potential buyers and lending institutions.

Participants in the secondary mortgage market who are considered to be important include those listed below: The Federal National Mortgage Association (often known as Fannie Mae) is an abbreviation that stands for Federal National Mortgage Association. Government-sponsored enterprises (GSEs), such as Fannie Mae, were formed by Congress in 1938. However, Fannie Mae is not a government-backed firm. It is a corporation in which the shareholders possess a majority stake. By acquiring mortgages from mortgage originators in the primary mortgage market, bundling them, and selling the resulting securities to investors, it supports them in expanding their operations and increasing their profits.

Fannie Mae's money in return for these mortgages is used to acquire further mortgages, bundle them, and engage in other similar operations. According to its mission statement, Fannie Mae was founded and continues to offer finance to the primary mortgage market to "improve the availability and affordability of homeownership and rental housing," according to its mission statement. Freddie Mac says, "I'm not going to lie to you, I'm not going to lie to you." Freddie Mac, like Fannie Mae, is a government-sponsored enterprise (GSE) that is owned by the investors who put their money into it. Congress established it in 1970 in order to enhance the amount of money that might be utilized for housing and, as a consequence, to improve "the liquidity, stability, and affordability of the United States housing market."

It operates similarly to Fannie Mae in that it is a government-sponsored company. Abbreviation for Government National Mortgage Association, Gennie Mae (Government National Mortgage Association) is an acronym for Government National Mortgage Association. While the other two GSEs are privately held corporations, Gennie Mae is a government-sponsored business that is a division of the Department of Housing and Urban Development. As an alternative to investing in or selling mortgages, the Federal Housing Administration (FHA) and the Department of Veterans Affairs (VA) guarantee mortgage-backed securities backed by government-insured or guaranteed loans (VA). (See the section on Mortgage Insurance Programs below for further information.) Gennie Mae provides pass-through securities as part of its mortgage-backed securities (MBS), which are securities that guarantee the monthly payment of principal and interest. Pass-through securities are securities that flow through to investors in mortgage-backed securities.

The acquisition, packaging, and sale of mortgages to investors are all made by private mortgage organizations, which are distinct from government-sponsored enterprises (such as Fannie Mae and Freddie Mac). Who are the purchasers of mortgage-backed securities (MBS) in the secondary mortgage market, and how do they make their purchases? Among the most popular purchasers of these securities are large pension funds, insurance companies, and hedge funds, which are investing organizations that cater to a small number of very wealthy clientele, such as the wealthy themselves. It is common for them to concentrate on high-risk investing prospects. In certain cases, buyers who put down less than 20% of the purchase price may be required to get mortgage insurance, depending on the specifics of the transaction.

The types of government contracts available are divided into two categories: public and private. The purpose of mortgage default insurance is to protect the lender from incurring a financial loss in the eve

nt that the mortgagor fails to make the mortgage payments. There should be no doubt about this: despite the fact that we often refer to these loans as "FHA mortgages" and "VA mortgages," neither the Federal Housing Administration (FHA) nor the Veterans Administration (VHA) really lend money. Unlike commercial lenders, such as credit unions, who issue mortgages, mortgage insurance is supplied only by government-sponsored enterprises (HUD). The Federal Housing Administration (FHA) will offer mortgage insurance to purchasers who meet certain requirements in some circumstances. Obtaining single-family or multifamily housing with no more than four units, with at least one of the units being utilized as an owner-occupied dwelling, is required in order to qualify.

The purchaser must use an FHA-approved lender and buy the property via an FHA-approved lender. Less than twenty percent of the property's worth is being paid as a down payment. It is vital to engage an appraiser whom the Federal Housing Administration has approved. The debt-to-income ratio meets the standards of the Federal Housing Administration (29 percent mortgage payment expense to effective income and 41 percent total fixed payment to effective income).

Loan constraints are based on the property's appraised value, and they differ from state to state and from county to county in their application. As part of the loan application process, the Federal Housing Administration assesses a fee of 2.25 percent of the loan amount, which is known as the mortgage insurance premium (MIP). Following then, the borrower will be obliged to pay an annual premium until the lender meets certain standards. At that point, the mortgagee is no longer liable for the insurance premiums that must be paid.

It is possible that home buyers who have less than 20% equity in their home may be compelled to get private mortgage insurance (PMI) from a private mortgage insurance company. In the case of a default by the mortgagor, private mortgage insurance (PMI) ensures that the lender will receive payment. The mortgagee is responsible for paying the PMI as part of the regular monthly mortgage payment. Mortgage insurance (PMI) must be automatically canceled when the equity in the home grows by more than 22 percent, as mandated by the federal Homeowners Protection Act of 1998, for mortgages signed on or after July 29, 1999, unless the borrower wishes otherwise. When a borrower is not current on their payments, the policy does not apply. It also applies only to private m

ortgage insurance (PMI), not to VA or FHA-insured mortgage loans. Some states have also passed laws related to PMI on their own initiative. As far as conventional mortgages are concerned, both Fannie Mae and Freddie Mac deal in them. Conventional mortgages are one of three types of loans offered to consumers: first mortgages, second mortgages, and third mortgages. This is a mortgage-backed real estate that is not insured nor guaranteed by any government agency. Traditional mortgages encompass numerous forms of home loans as well as all nonresidential loans, such as construction loans, which are examples of conventional loans. Conventional loans also include personal loans and business loans.

Conforming mortgage

Freddie Mac and Fannie Mae accept conforming mortgages guaranteed by the Federal National Mortgage Association and are suitable for sale to Freddie Mac and Fannie Mae. The amount of the mortgage cannot exceed the annual adjusted dollar barrier established by the Federal Reserve in any one year.

In 2009, the most you could expect to pay for a single-family home was $417,000 USD. The mortgage must also contain some universal terms that Fannie Mae and Freddie Mac specify. A mortgage that does not comply with the conditions of the loan is referred to as a defaulted mortgage. There are a variety of reasons why nonconforming mortgages are ineligible for sale to Fannie Mae or Freddie Mac, including the fact that the loan amount exceeds a certain threshold, the fact that the mortgagee has a poor credit rating, the fact that adequate documentation is lacking, and the fact that the mortgage does not contain the standard provisions required by Fannie Mae and Freddie Mac.

Mortgages with fixed rates and terms of 30 years were historically the most prevalent sort. However, as the banking industry got more deregulated, lenders developed new ways to profit from the money they lent out. Homebuyers now have a variety of mortgage alternatives to select from, depending on their credit score and the amount of money they can put down as a down payment on their new home.

The interest rate on a fixed-rate mortgage remains the same for the term of the loan, as makes the amount of money owed each month under the loan. A fixed-rate mortgage is one that has a fixed term of 15, 20, or 30 years, depending on the lending institution. Depending on whom you ask, this kind of loan is referred to as a conventional mortgage in certain sectors. Variable-rate mortgages (also known as adjustable-rate mortgages (ARMs)) have interest rates that are susceptible to change from time to time, while fixed-rate mortgages do not. Changes in the yield on the 10-year Treasury bill or the prime rate have an effect on the interest rate. It is unnecessary for you to understand the ins and outs of the policy driving these changes. It is sufficient for you to understand that the Federal Reserve's policies can cause a rise or fall in short-term interest rates and, as a result, a rise or fall in the mortgage rates that your buyers will be required to pay, as described above.

An important issue when selecting whether to purchase an ARM and what kind of ARM to obtain is the index used to calculate changes in interest rates (for example, 1-year Treasury rates, London Interbank Offered Rate (LIBOR), or Costs of Funds Index (COFI), among other things. The margin, which is indicated as a percentage of the index, represents the revenue received by the lender from the loan. Interest rate caps, which are described as a restriction on the amount by which a lender may raise interest rates, are defined in the following ways: an annual cap on the amount of money you can spend (typically by no more than 2 percent points). There are many different ARM configurations to choose from, including Standard ARM architecture consists of the following components: As long as the loan is for a specified length of time, the interest rate will fluctuate on a monthly, semiannual, or annual basis throughout its tenure, depending on the terms of the loan.

Nonetheless, the mortgagee is only paying interest payments, not principal payments, with each installment of the mortgage payment schedule. At the end of the mortgage's term, the borrower is obligated to make a single payment that pays the whole principal sum owed on loan. Convertible adjustable-rate mortgages (ARMs) are a kind of mortgage in which the borrower has the option of switching from an ARM to a fixed-rate mortgage after a certain period of time has passed. The new interest rate is computed as specified in the initial adjustable-rate mortgage (ARM), also known as an introductory rate mortgage. At the time of conversion, the mortgagor is obliged to pay a fee to the lender. An ARM with a fixed rate and interest-only: this kind of loan has an initial period when your bank remits just the interest, and afterward the loan is terminated. It is common in this situation for the mortgage to be amortized over a shorter payback time and for the payment amount to be raised, typically considerably, in order to ensure that the whole mortgage balance is paid off at the end of the mortgage's term.

There are two basic types of mortgages: fixed-rate mortgages and adjustable-rate mortgages. However, a variety of characteristics can be found in mortgages that may make them more suitable for certain borrowers than pure fixed-rate mortgages or pure adjustable-rate mortgages, depending on the borrower's situation. Here are a few illustrations: at the end of the loan's term, usually 5 or 7 years, the borrower must pay the entire outstanding balance.

A balloon loan is a type of mortgage in which the borrower makes monthly payments equal to a predetermined amount for the loan duration, typically 5 or 7 years. The borrower is required to pay the entire outstanding balance. The most significant distinction between a balloon ARM and a standard ARM is that the monthly payments are set for the loan duration. For loans that do not self-amortize, which means that the amount owing is not paid in full at the end of the term, a balloon payment is needed at the end of the term. Rather than paying off the loan once a month, the mortgagor pays off the debt every two weeks, which is called a biweekly loan. Even though the installments are half the amount of a monthly payment, the mortgagee is still obligated to make an interest payment once a year on their mortgage (26 payments versus 12 payments).

Straight-term mortgage

A straight-term mortgage, also known as an interest-only mortgage, requires the mortgagor to pay only the interest on the loan during the life of the loan, with the whole loan amount due at the end of the loan term. Straight-term mortgages are also known as interest-only loans. When a loan is deemed open, it is feasible to pay it off early without incurring a prepayment penalty on the part of the mortgagor.

A mortgage with an open end that is for a certain period of time: this is a mortgage that allows the mortgagor to borrow more money under the same mortgage provided certain criteria are satisfied; these terms are often tied to the mortgagor's assets. This kind of mortgage is most commonly seen in second mortgages.

Package mortgage

A buyer who is acquiring not just real estate but also personal things inside the home, such as furniture, in addition to the real estate would use this technique. Purchase-money mortgage (sometimes known as a purchase money loan): this kind of loan, which is also known as seller financing or owner financing, is used to finance the acquisition of a house. The buyer borrows from the seller instead of borrowing from a financial institution or borrowing from a financial institution. It may be necessary for a buyer to employ this kind of mortgage if they do not meet the requirements for a traditional loan in its totality. As part of a shared equity financing arrangement, a potential homeowner borrows money to make the down payment, and in return, the lender obtains a piece of the property's market value as recompense.

Upon the sale of the property, the lender gets a portion of the profit in proportion to the amount of money that the lender borrowed to acquire the property. For example, the utilization of shared equity to buy a home by parents aiding an adult child or newlyweds might be an example of shared equity. According to the state, if the parents wish to purchase a property, they would need to qualify for a mortgage as well as be on the mortgage and deed.

Mortgage with graduated payments (GPM)

Even though the interest rate is fixed, the payments start out small and steadily increase over time. Initial installments are insufficient to meet interest charges. The amount of the payment difference is added to the total amount of the loan obligation. Borrowers that fulfill the requirements depending on the size of their first payment may be given a GPM contract.

Growing equity mortgage (GEM)

When you use the GEM, the increases are applied solely to the principal amount of the loan, not to any additional amounts. According to the lender, this kind of mortgage may be good for folks who are just starting out and expect their income to increase over time. A wraparound mortgage is when the buyer receives a loan that includes the remaining amount on the seller's mortgage. The buyer makes payments to their lender that include payments on the seller's original mortgage as part of the payments.

The new lender then reimburses the original seller's mortgagee in the transaction. The term refers to a kind of refinancing in which the new loan is ranked second to the existing debt but is still considered an obligation of the borrower, as opposed to the opposite. Whenever a buyer does not have the cash on hand to complete the transaction right immediately, a temporary loan, also known as a bridge loan or a swing loan, is used to bridge the gap until the necessary funds are made available. Suppose a buyer has to sell their existing property in order to finance the purchase of a new house, but closing on the current property has been delayed due to unanticipated circumstances. A bridge loan would be used in this situation, among other situations. According to the National Mortgage Association, businesses are more likely than individuals to make use of specific types of mortgages and property financing.

A blanket mortgage is a loan that is secured by more than one piece of real estate and is referred to as such. This kind of financing is often used in the construction of subdivisions. Whenever a mortgage has a partial release clause, it allows a builder to develop and sell individual lots, with each sale representing a portion of the mortgage debt being paid off.

A construction loan of this kind provides financing for construction projects at different stages of the project's lifespan, such as during the development phase. Taking up a construction loan to build a single-family home or a housing complex are both viable choices for homebuilders. As opposed to a standard mortgage, sale-and-leaseback finance is a kind of financing for commercial activities rather than a residential mortgage. The seller of a property agrees to continue to reside in the property as a tenant of the new owner after the sale is completed. For their personal use, the original owner maintains the value of the property, whilst the new owner is assured a specific amount of rent for a certain period of time.

Purchase of a mortgage rate reduction

Even though it is not a mortgage, this is a kind of financing that developers often provide to consumers who are purchasing new construction. The plan is similar to a subsidy in that it aids the purchaser is paying a part of the monthly mortgage payment during the first year or two after purchasing the property. The subprime mortgage defaults that rattled the world's economy beginning in 2007 served as a trigger for the global financial crisis that began in 2008 and continues today.

The term "subprime mortgage" refers to a kind of loan that is made accessible to those who have low credit records and would otherwise be unable to get a mortgage. Mortgage lenders charge high interest rates to this category of borrowers in order to compensate for the greater chance of loan defaults associated with this group of borrowers. Many of the most exotic mortgages, such as monthly-variable adjustable-rate mortgages (ARMs) and mortgages with low teaser rates (beginning rates), are only accessible via subprime lending institutions.

A number of companies that provided subprime loans during the heyday of subprime lending have been accused by the federal government of participating in predatory lending practices, which they vigorously dispute. Despite the fact that several subprime lenders have closed their doors, there are still subprime mortgages accessible on the market. Buyers who put off applying for a mortgage until their credit has improved will save a considerable amount of money on interest payments in the long run. Mortgagees are permitted to get new mortgages on top of their current ones if the terms of their initial loan do not limit

mortgage" refers to a second mortgage, while the term "senior
...age on a property. If a buyer eventually defaults on the senior
...entitled to receive repayment first, before any future (junior)
...eserve Board has a significant influence on the mortgage industry,
...part from that, the United States Congress has passed legislation to protect consumers who obtain mortgage credit. In addition, the Department of Housing and Urban Development and other federal agencies have established rules and regulations governing mortgage originators, including their obligations to borrowers, among other things. It is the Real Estate Settlement Procedures Act (RESPA) that controls the settlement of real estate transactions on a federal level. It was phased between January 2009 and January 2010 that the present laws and regulations that implement RESPA became effective. They apply to all residential acquisitions for which a mortgage loan is obtained by the residential purchaser, as well as all residential refinancing transactions. The present laws and regulations that implement RESPA were phased in over a two-year period, beginning in January 2009 and ending in January 2010.

To a certain degree, a variant of this form is also used in small commercial real estate transactions as a convenient way to keep track of the costs associated with the loan as well. "Loan originators must provide borrowers with a standard Good Faith Estimate that clearly discloses essential loan conditions and closing fees, and closing agents must present borrowers with a new HUD-1 settlement statement," according to the law, which also requires, among other things, that loan originators provide borrowers with a standard Good Faith Estimate that clearly discloses essential loan conditions and closing fees.

Truth-in-Lending Act

It is known as the Consumer Credit Protection Act and regulates certain disclosures for mortgage loans, including the amount of fees and charges that must be declared, the method in which mortgage financing must be offered, and information about variable-rate mortgages. Customers who apply for an adjustable-rate mortgage must get specified information, which is mandated by federal statute.

With the goal of encouraging banks as well as other depository institutions to "assist in having met the credit needs of the communities in which it operates, particularly those located in low- as well as moderate-income neighborhoods," The Community Reinvestment Act was enacted in 1977 and has been amended several times since then, the most recent amendment being in 2005. This includes the creation of mortgage loans for eligible buyers, if applicable. As a result of the Equal Credit Opportunity Act, it is illegal to discriminate in any credit transaction, even when applying for a home loan.

The Fair Housing Act

Discrimination in the acquisition and financing of residential real estate is prohibited under this regulation. When the Great Recession of 2007-09 hit, many Americans learned the hard way that if you don't keep up with your mortgage payments on a regular basis, you run the danger of losing your home to foreclosure. Generally speaking, foreclosures may be divided into three groups:

Foreclosure via the courts

When a mortgagee files a petition with the court seeking a foreclosure order, the court sets a timeframe by which the mortgagor must pay off the mortgage amount in full or face legal consequences. If the mortgagor cannot meet the deadline, the court orders that the property has to be sold at an auction to satisfy the debt. When a lienholder receives less money than is necessary to pay off the mortgage after subtracting court fees and other related costs, they may be able to get a deficiency judgment against the mortgagor (and additional liens).

Simple foreclosure

In this approach, the mortgagee goes to court and secures an order requiring the payment of the mortgage as well as a date by which the mortgage payments will no longer be required to be made. Mortgagees become the legal owners of a property as soon as they obtain full payment on a mortgage. The mortgagor's rights to a property are terminated when a mortgagee gets payment in full.

To settle the lien on the property, the mortgagee may elect to retain the property rather than sell it. In certain states, foreclosures under stringent terms are not authorized, yet in others, they are. When a mortgagee misses on their payments, the lender sells the property without going through the regular foreclosure procedure. Although the mortgagee is obligated to serve notice on the overdue homeowner first, this is not always the case. If the borrower is unable to pay off the mortgage, the mortgagee may be entitled to sell the property to recover the money owed to them.

Chapter 11: Leasing

A lease is a legal arrangement that establishes the ownership of a leasehold property. The term "lease" refers to a written agreement between a lessor (landlord) and a lessee (tenant) that is normally for a certain period and for a particular amount (rent), and which is signed by both parties. When a lease is for one year or longer, the majority of jurisdictions require that the agreement has to be in writing; the state's Statute of Frauds controls this. State governments and some municipalities have also passed additional laws, rules, and regulations to govern the landlord-tenant relationship, which are listed below. The rules that regulate rent control are explored in further detail below.

Originally published in 1972, the Uniform Residential Landlord and Tenant Act was intended to serve as a model for state legislation by the National Conference of Commissioners on Uniform State Laws (National Conference of Commissioners on Uniform State Laws). Many states have accepted its provisions, either in whole or in part. It's crucial to note that even when a property is sold, the lease remains to be in effect. Purchasing an apartment building with tenants who are still under the terms of their existing leases and the conditions of their contracts, which may include the amount of rent they pay, gives you the right to keep them in the building. (There may be certain exceptions to this rule in the case of commercial leasing agreements.) When it comes to rental leases, there are many more criteria than are required in order for it to be called a legally binding agreement. Typically, a lease will include the terms and conditions listed below.

Terms & Conditions

The property's address and description are provided in the package. The names of the persons who signed the lease are shown below. The amount of time that the lease will be in effect (time period), the amount of rent that must be paid, as well as the date by which it must be paid are listed. Any rent increases that occur during the course of the lease's duration (a two-year lease, for example, might have one amount for year one and another amount, due to an increase, for year 2). A late fee will be applied if the rent is not paid on time, and the day on which the late fee is levied will be included on the rent bill as well.

The amount of the security deposit, where it is maintained when it is returned to the tenant, how much of it may be retained by the landlord, and under what circumstances are all covered in detail.

No matter whether the landlord or the renter is responsible for the utilities, what can be done with the premises (limits the use of the premises to specific purposes, such as use as a residence; the tenant would then not be allowed to open a retail outlet in the living room or convert a clothing boutique into a restaurant).

Whether or not the landlord or tenant is responsible for liability insurance, and if so, what level of coverage is necessary. To understand who is liable for different sorts of repairs (and how this relates to other problems that may arise in a lease, such as the terms under which a landlord may get access to the premises and the tenant's right to quiet enjoyment), it is necessary to review the lease. To what extent the renter is entitled to renovate or improve their rental property (typically, the tenant, if allowed to make changes, must return the place to the condition in which the tenant received it).

In the case that the premises are destroyed, the tenants' and landlord's responsibilities are clearly defined. The information you need to know about renewing your lease (nonrenewable, automatic renewal, or renewal with notice to the landlord). Upon surrender, the premises must be in the same condition as when they were received, or they must have "reasonable wear and tear" on them, whichever is more. Additional limitations may include a ban on pets or a limit on the number of pets that may be kept on the premises. According to the courts, renters also have the right to quiet enjoyment (i.e., the capacity to use the premises without fear of being sued by others), whether or not this is specifically stated in the lease. A tenant may be permitted to sublet or assign the premises with authorization from the landlord under certain leases, while others may expressly forbid such action. The original tenant retains the right to retake control of the premises from the new tenant when a certain period of time has elapsed under the terms of the sublease agreement.

In a legal arrangement, the previous tenant relinquishes all ownership rights to the property, and the new renter becomes the new owner. There is no way that any of these agreements will result in the original tenant being relieved of any of their contractual responsibilities. The original tenant ultimately must pay the rent and fulfill all other tenant obligations and responsibilities under the lease, not the responsibility of any subtenants or assignments. Also stated in the agreement is that the sublease is responsible for adhering to all of the terms and conditions set out in the tenant's lease and will not violate any of those terms or provisions. Subletting also commits the sublease to the conditions of their landlord's lease, which means that if the tenant is evicted, the sublease will be required to vacate the premises at the same time.

A lease option, sometimes known as a lease buy option, is a word that refers to a purchase option on a lease. It allows the renter to purchase the property at any moment throughout the term of the lease agreement, if they so desire.

The leasing agreement specifies the amount that will be charged for the lease. It may be feasible to deduct a portion of each month's rent from the purchase price. The renter also pays a non-refundable choice deposit, which is used toward the purchase price in addition to the rental payment. An option must be exercised in strict conformity with the terms of the contract in order to be valid. An additional option open to long-term tenants, especially those who want to make considerable repairs to the home, is the "right of first refusal." Individuals who want to invest substantial money in home improvements are especially fond of this choice. Whenever a landlord decides to sell a property, the lease provision would state that the property will first be offered to the tenant, and if the landlord receives a good faith offer to purchase the property from someone else, the tenant will have the right to purchase the property if they meet the terms of that offer. A landlord's choice of the lease is usually dictated by one of two factors: the kind of property that is being rented out, and the technique used to decide how much rent to charge. The following are the most common types of real estate leases that you may encounter.

Gross lease

A gross lease is the most prevalent kind of apartment leasing arrangement. When signing a lease, a tenant agrees to make monthly payments of the same amount of rent for a defined length of time, known as the lease's tenure. To be eligible for this, the landlord must agree to be responsible for paying real estate taxes, doing regular maintenance and repairs, carrying out renovations, and acquiring liability insurance for the property in exchange. A tenant or a landlord may be liable for paying utilities, depending on the conditions of their lease agreement. A lease for office space may work similarly to that described above. Net leases are the most often used kind of commercial real estate rental agreement in the commercial real estate rental market.

In addition to the base fee, the renter is responsible for a portion or all of the expenses connected with the property, including but not limited to maintenance and utilities. Depending on how much of the tenant's expenses, a net lease may be referred to as a double net lease, triple net lease, or an absolute net lease. In the case of an absolute net lease, for example, the tenant is liable for all utilities, repair and maintenance expenses, as well as real estate taxes. Renters are also liable for the expense of replacing the roof of the building if the roof has to be replaced for any reason.

Percentage lease

When compared to a net lease, a percentage lease is comparable in the sense that the renter is accountable for base rent. Tenants are also expected to pay a share of the revenues produced by their businesses to their landlords, as described above. It is common for retailers, such as stores in malls and shopping centers, to employ retail leases, which are a kind of lease that is used for retail leasing. Depending on the percentage leasing agreement, the base rent may or may not be subtracted from the total amount payable. In addition to having a percentage lease, it is possible to have a retail lease that is either a gross or net lease, which implies that the tenant can choose whether or not to pay for part or all of the operating expenses connected with the premises. A ground lease, which is also known as a land lease, is a kind of rental agreement in which a piece of unimproved land is leased with the expectation that the tenant would build a structure on the property over the life of the lease. Ground leases are often multi-year, long-term arrangements with a landowner that last for a number of years. An example of a lessee is a developer who signs a 99-year lease with a real estate holding company in order to construct a retail Centre on the holding company's land.

As soon as the lease period ends, the holding company (landlord) will assume ownership of both the buildings and the surrounding land, becoming the legal owner of the property. During this time period, the tenant is liable for all retail center expenses, including real estate taxes, water and sewer fees, maintenance, and other costs. The amount of rent paid may be fixed or may be dependent on a percentage of the business's total sales revenue.

Graduated lease

A graded lease is a long-term lease that is divided into many years of payments. While the rent for a graded lease is not set like the rent for a ground lease, the rent for a graded leasing arrangement is. There are two ways for determining rent for the purposes of evaluating it. Depending on how the assessed value of the premises changes over time, it may be essential to adjust the rent.

Alternatively, it may be necessary to adjust the rent according to a benchmark rate, such as the consumer price index, to keep pace with inflation. States, counties, and municipalities have the right to create legislation that controls the amount of rent that landlords may charge tenants in their respective jurisdictions, and this authority extends to the amount of rent that landlords may charge renters in their respective jurisdictions.

Rent control restrictions may not apply to some kinds of apartments, such as two-family dwellings and new construction, depending on the state in which they are located. Most rent laws outline the landlord's responsibility for providing heat and hot water and for doing repairs, and they outline the procedures for evicting tenants, among other things.

Landlords are vocal in their opposition to rent limits, and they have been effective in persuading governments to change or overturn the legislation. Those who have lived in the same unit for a long length of time are the most important beneficiaries of rent control legislation. Despite the fact that they may be paying as little as $400 per month for an apartment in a prestigious location, flats in the same building that are no longer subject to rent control rent for as much as $1,500 per month on the free market. Because of the lack of control over vacancy, the difference in rent is permitted in this case.

A tenant who was previously subject to rent control vacates the premises, and rent control for the unit is discontinued, and the landlord may charge the current market rate for the unit. Many states and municipalities also have their own rent stabilization legislation, which are in effect.

The majority of the time, a rent-stabilized apartment means that the landlord may only raise the rent by a specified percentage per year, and the tenant has the choice to renew the lease when it expires, as long as the rate is not increased. Rental properties that are exempt from regulation under rent stabilization legislation, just as they are under rent control legislation, may also be free from regulation under rent control legislation. A tenant takes new employment and is forced to relocate, but they still have eight months left on their current rental agreement. The tenant can seek to get a sub lessee, or an assignee of the lease enables it; nevertheless, there is a high possibility that the lease does not provide for this remedy in this scenario. The only other option available is to cancel the lease agreement in its entirety. The renter will very probably lose their security deposit in lieu of paying a full month's rent, even though it is anticipated that the tenant and the landlord would come to an amicable agreement.

A tenant is judged to have abandoned the lease if the landlord and tenant are unable to come to an agreement on the terms of its termination. In this case, the tenant forfeits the security deposit, which is returned to the landlord. Apart from that, a landlord is entitled to sue for damages, which may include the loss of rental income.

Tenant and landlord separations that are not amicable include actual eviction, constructive eviction, and retaliatory eviction, to name a few scenarios. Eviction is the process of removing a tenant from a property and transferring control of the property back to the property's owner.

The most typical causes that result in a tenant's actual eviction from a property include nonpayment of rent by the tenant, a tenant's refusal to vacate the premises after the lease has expired (known as a "holdover tenant," and a tenant's continuous violation of other lease terms.

Theft of property is another issue that may necessitate a person's departure from the location. There are three phases to eviction proceedings:

- Filing a complaint with the court to get an eviction notice.
- Serving the tenant with the notice.
- Holding a hearing to gather evidence from both sides of a legal dispute.

If the landlord's case is upheld, the tenant will be served with a warrant for the repossession of the property and will be compelled to depart the premises immediately. To put it simply, this is the procedure that is followed when a tenant is evicted or expelled from their property. It is possible to be evicted constructively if your landlord fails to maintain your property, resulting in it being uninhabitable for you and your fellow renters. In this specific scenario, the tenant has the option to vacate the premises and cancel the lease agreement.

For example, a plumbing leak between floors destroys the kitchen equipment in a tenant's lower apartment, leaving them inoperable and prohibiting the renter from preparing or refrigerating food for the remainder of the month. The landlord is refusing to fix the leak on the premises. The most prevalent causes for constructive eviction are a lack of heat or water and insufficient or non-existent care of the property in question.

Eviction as a form of retaliation

A tenant has been evicted from a rental property in violation of state and local laws. Consider the following scenario: in the prior example, the tenant filed a complaint with the appropriate municipal agency about the landlord's failure to repair the faulty plumbing, and the agency investigated the problem.

After receiving no aid from the local authorities, the landlord retaliates by turning off all water to the apartment.

The tenant is compelled to move as a result of this action. This is a retaliatory eviction, and the landlord may be subject to criminal prosecution as a consequence of the action taken against him.

Apart from recruiting tenants for landlords, some real estate brokers and agents also serve as property managers for those landlords who use their services. Except for those who manage apartment complexes, all property managers are needed to have a valid real estate license, regardless of whether or not the state mandates such licensing. Both the realtor and the landlord must sign a contract detailing the services that the realtor will provide in their position as a property manager before the realtor may begin managing the property. There is a variety of them, including the following: Searching for appropriate renters, which involves advertising for tenants and checking references, is a time-consuming and difficult task. Lease discussions are a typical event in the real estate industry. Rent is being collected on a daily basis. Involvement with or supervision of individuals and enterprises involved in property maintenance and cleaning services, landscape design and maintenance, waste disposal, security, accounting, and other related services.

Participating in eviction procedures on the landlord's behalf in a professional capacity as remuneration for their services, the property manager may get a percentage of the rental income or a fixed fee for maintaining the payments schedule. The amount of remuneration depends on the services that are provided by the management when compensation is specified as a percentage.

Chapter 12: Transferring Ownership: Deeds and Title Closing

A real estate transaction is completed when the ownership of a piece of property is transferred from one person to another. This is the climax of your efforts as a real estate agent.

As a result of the transaction, you will most likely only get compensation if the property is sold or exchanged and ownership of the property is transferred due to that transaction. To be clear, another phrase in real estate jargon implies the same thing as transferred, and I use the term conveyed interchangeably with the word transferred when referring to a transfer of ownership. According to the perspective of a real estate agent, after a contract has been signed, several further processes must be completed by either the agent or both the agent and legal counsel in order to transfer ownership of the property from one party to the other party. Throughout this chapter, learn important information regarding how property ownership is transferred from one person to another.

My discussion of property ownership includes the paperwork that is necessary, such as the deed, as well as how property is defined so that there are no misconceptions about who owns something and who does not own it. An additional topic covered in the process of "title closure," which is the process through which ownership of real estate is formally transferred from one person to another. In the context of real estate, the term "title" refers to the possession of the property.

Therefore, rather than using the phrase ownership to indicate when ownership has been transferred, the majority of people in the real estate sector say something along the lines of "The title was conveyed on Tuesday." In contrast to the title to a vehicle, the title to a vehicle is not a legally binding document. No matter what circumstances surround the transfer of property ownership from one person to another, the phrases convey, and transfer are used to denote how property ownership is transferred. The scenarios in which the title is transmitted or transferred include a gift, a sale, and an exchange. The deed, which acts as a legal document that transfers ownership of a piece of property from one person to another, is one of the most important pieces of paper a person may have. In addition to serving as a permanent record of your property ownership for the life of your possession or until you transfer title to someone else, it is crucial because it is the first step in the transfer of title.

To the extent possible, the material in this part is designed to provide you with a knowledge of the exact circumstances and terminology that must be contained in a deed in order for it to be considered legal. I also go through additional wording in the deed that might have an effect on how you utilize the property, and I give you an overview of the numerous kinds of deeds that are available. As well as information on how real estate is presented, this part offers information that might assist you in understanding who owns what and avoiding any potential ambiguity.

The statute of fraud is a piece of law that has been implemented in every state to acknowledge the need to establish and show property ownership in a legal environment. According to the statute of fraud, all real estate title transfers must be completed in writing to avoid liability. However, regardless of where you reside in the state, the basic elements for a valid deed, and hence a genuine transfer, are typically the same. The following criteria are listed in the general order in which they appear in most deeds, except the last requirement listed in the reverse order. This person is known as the grantor and is the current owner of a property who is transferring ownership of the property to another party. Before a grant is evaluated, the grantor must be of legal age and have the necessary legal capacity. It is a good idea to double-check your state's legal age of competence, even though it is unlikely that you would be asked a particular question regarding your age of legal competency during an interview. Keep in mind that the donor may be planning to sell the property or donate it to a charitable organization.

12.1 Grantee

The grantee is the person who will be awarded legal ownership of the property when it has been granted to them. The identification of the grantee is one of the most important considerations when drafting a will, as it ensures that there is no confusion about who you are dealing with when the time comes to distribute the estate. The grantee's name should be reflected in the deed if the grantor's name is John Smith III, especially if the grantor's parents, John Smith I and John

II, are still living. In certain cases, it is also important to provide the addresses of both the donor and the beneficiary. A legitimate deed must contain wording that suggests that the grantor is receiving something of value in exchange for the property being transferred if the deed is to be considered valid. Generally, money is being received, and the consideration clause must state how much money has been received in order to be effective.

Certain settings make use of the phrase "ten dollars and other valuable consideration" or anything along those lines to express the amount of the consideration being offered. The number of times individuals have come up to me after examining a deed that contained the words "What a fantastic bargain the buyer must have gotten" is beyond count. In the event that someone intends to keep the true amount of money spent on the property disguised, the reference to ten dollars may be used to hide such information from the general public.

Clause awarding ownership

Upon signing the document, a giving clause says that the grantor is transferring ownership of a piece of real estate to the grantee and that the grantee is receiving the property. In fact, in certain areas, the granting clause is referred to as the conditions of transfer rather than the granting clause. Among the provisions of the deed is wording that makes it clear exactly what rights are being transferred to the grants and if the grants are acquiring title to the property jointly with another person.

The habendum clause, which is composed of the terms "to have" and "to possess," goes on to clarify the concepts of having and possessing rights in further detail. The habendum clause goes into further detail on the rights that are being granted to the grantee. If you've already been married, the habendum clause may seem a little like you're being married all over again, which may be good or bad.

There must be consistency between the language used in the habendum clause and the language used in the granting clause for the clause to be valid. Including a habendum clause may change from one jurisdiction to another since it must be compatible with the granting clause in any situation, regardless of the jurisdiction.

Description in legalese

At this point, consider the legal description included within this section to be language meant to ensure that there is no confusion about the specific borders of the property that is being transferred. The following are examples of exceptions and reservations:

Signature of the grantor

The grantor's signature is required in order for the deed to be considered valid. Generally speaking, if more than one person holds a property, all owners must sign the deed. In certain states, even though the spouse does not hold title to the property, a husband or wife who owns property on their own may be compelled to have the spouse sign the deed as a cosigner. An attorney-in-fact may sign a deed on behalf of a client in the majority of states and jurisdictions across the world. In order to sign a deed, an attorney-in-fact must be appointed by a power of attorney, which is a legal document signed by someone allowing another person the authority to act on his or her behalf in a specific situation. On the other hand, an attorney-in-fact does not have to be a lawyer to perform his or her duties. In certain states, a third party must sign the deed to attest that the grantor is the person who signed the deed and not someone else. This is done to protect the grantor's identity. If the donor is a corporation, on the other hand, there may be extra conditions to be met. In order to transfer property managed by a company to another party, a resolution by the corporate board of directors or a majority vote of the shareholders is often necessary. The deed must be signed by one or more corporate executives whom the business's board of directors has duly authorized.

Acknowledgement: In the legal world, an acknowledgement is a way of establishing that the person who signed a deed did so voluntarily and that he is, in fact, who he claims to be.

Notary publics are often used to witness and attest to acknowledgements. You must provide identification and indicate that you are signing the document of your own free will in front of a notary public before the document may be acknowledged. A deed does not need to contain an acknowledgment in order to be valid in theory; but, in most states, a deed that does not include an acknowledgment will not be recorded in the official public records and will be null and invalid. Keep in mind that it is not always necessary to record a deed in order for a transfer of ownership to be legal, however, it is usually a good idea. Even if it's a wonderful notion, it's not necessary in any manner.

Transfer of title by delivery and acceptance

Until the deed is handed to the grantee and accepted by him or her, the transfer of ownership of real estate is not regarded to have taken place.

"Passing title" refers to the acts of transferring ownership of a deed from one person to another. The day on which ownership is transferred is the same day on which the deed was provided and accepted by the other party. When a transaction is completed in escrow, there is an exception to this requirement in certain jurisdictions. Briefly stated, when the deed is delivered to the escrow agency, title is transferred. Unfortunately, there are a number of different forms of deeds, which I'm sorry to say will frustrate you as a real estate investor. I'm sure you were hoping that there would be just one type of deed. While all deeds convey ownership, they differ in the sorts of warranties or guarantees that they provide to the receiver, which may be advantageous or damaging to the grantee.

Despite the fact that a formal deed is not required, many deeds include provisions for different assurances granted by the grantor to the new owner, which are not required. Different types of deeds may be used based on a variety of variables, including the identity of the grantor of the property and the reason for the transfer of the property. These factors are generally those that lawyers like addressing, although most states need their real estate brokers to have at least a basic awareness of the many types of deeds in order to sell real estate.

And, while we're on the topic of states, you'll want to check into the most common types of deeds used in your state to see whether they have names that differ from the ones I've listed. If they do, you'll want to make a note of them. Your relicense course, the textbook you are currently reading, and any handouts provided by your instructor will all include this information.

While studying this section in preparation for the exam, keep in mind that you can generally tell the difference between one kind of deed and another by the various guarantees provided and the various reasons for why the deeds are used. Furthermore, the writers of state exams want you to be acquainted with just the most essential concepts and information. Even though you may have several questions that you need to ask your lawyer, you shouldn't be worried about them during the exam since they will be addressed during the exam itself. The following sections provide in-depth descriptions of a variety of acts and their consequences. General warranty deeds, sometimes known as general warranty agreements, are legal documents that guarantee the performance of a product or service. When it comes to addressing title concerns in the future, the grantor undertakes to fund all of the costs connected with the process. One characteristic of general warranty deeds stands out: the warranties cover any title concerns that may have developed throughout the tenure of all prior owners, regardless of when the deed was recorded. An important factor in explaining why a general warranty deed offers the greatest level of title protection to the grantee is that it provides the most complete set of assurances and that the grantor is held fully and solely responsible for all former owners' activities pertaining to title problems.

When it comes to special warranty deeds, only two types of warranties are covered. The first thing to keep in mind is that the grantor is the legal owner of the property. Second, it is a pledge that no damage was done to the title while the grantor was in possession, and that, in the event that a problem did arise, the grantor would correct it as soon as possible. When comparing a specific warranty deed to a general warranty deed, the most significant differences are the number of promises contained in the deed and the fact that the grantor is accountable for things that happened only while he was in possession of the property. Depending on the state, the special warranty deed may also be referred to as a bargain and sale deed, and it may have restrictions on the grantor's ability to engage in specific activities in particular areas, such as real estate development. Third parties may utilize special warranty deeds to protect themselves against the restrictions of the promises that have been issued. For example, the executor of an estate may use a special warranty deed to transfer property that belongs to the estate or trust to a beneficiary whom the executor has designated.

Grant deeds are used in a few states, and they provide very limited warranties on the property that is being given to the recipient. If the grantor later obtains any other title to the property, the grantee will also receive a copy of the other title. This deed ensures that the property has not been sold or otherwise transferred to anyone else, and that there are no restrictions on the use of the property other than those specifically listed in the deed. These guarantees are only effective for the period of time that the grantor was the legal owner of the property at the time of the donation.

However, even if the grant deed is only used in a few states, you should be aware of the following information if yours happens to be one of them. Compared to other forms of conveyance, this type of document is distinguished by the absence of assurances. On the surface, it seems that the grantor has entire possession of the property. In essence, the agreement does not provide any protection to the grantee (receiver of the title to the property). The deed may include warranties to make it more similar to the special warranty deed, in which case it is referred to as a bargain and sale deed with a covenant against grantors' actions.

The grantee is not bound by any statements or guarantees made by the grantor, and there is no inference drawn from the quitclaim deed as to how much or how secure the grantor's ownership of the land is. It only transfers the amount of ownership interest that the grantor may have in the property to the beneficiary. There is no additional ownership interest transferred as a result of this transaction.

Quitclaim papers are often used to resolve any problems in a property's title that have arisen over time. Any situation where there is something that makes the title appear less than complete, such as someone who appears to be occupying the property without the owner's permission, or something that indicates that another ownership interest may exist, such as two properties that are adjacent to each other and both claim to be the owners of a private road, can result in a cloud on the title. Quitclaim deeds are sometimes used for simple transfers of property ownership within a family, such as when a parent dies away, but they are seldom utilized for more complicated transfers. As well as being known by the terms "deed of trust" and "deed in trust," the term "trust deed" refers to a legal instrument that transfers ownership of property from one party to another for the benefit of a beneficiary in return for the payment of a debt. As an example, consider the following: A trust deed is signed by PARTY A, the trustor, in exchange for a loan from PARTY

B, the lender. The trust deed transfers ownership of the property for which the loan was received to Party C, the trustee, and a third party. The lender is the only one who will benefit from the loan. In the event that Party A pays back the whole amount of money that was lent to the lender, Party C will cede title of the property to Party A, and the transaction will be completed. When Party A fails to meet his or her financial obligations, Party C sells the property and transfers the earnings to the lender, who uses the cash to pay off the debt. A conveyance deed is used in a similar manner to transfer ownership of property from a trustee to a trustor when a debt for which the property acts as security has been fulfilled. Any time that the trustee transfers ownership of property held by the trust to another party, a trustee's deed is executed by them on behalf of the trust.

Consider the situation of a young child who owns property that is held in trust for him until he reaches the age of majority in the United States. Alternatively, suppose the trust decides to sell the property. In that case, the trustee may use a trustee's deed to transfer title of the property to a third-party beneficiary, which is a legal document.

Deeds are often issued after legal proceedings have been completed. For example, an executor's deed in the case of a deceased person's estate and a sheriff's deed in the case of a sale of property that has been seized by a local unit of government or a financial institution are both examples of deeds that a court orders. These deeds are created by state law, and the manner in which they are executed is likewise determined by state legislation. You should get acquainted with this topic even though you are unlikely to face many questions on it on your state exam, just in case you do.

When it comes to specifying the borders of a piece of land, a deed must be as specific as possible. For the most part, the rationale for this being so important is clear. The point at which you get to the end of your own territory is when you will find yourself on the edge of crossing over into another country's territory.

Consider the alternative: having one's own automobile. My car's look and the place where it is parked are both well-established in my mind. There are no doubts about where the vehicle begins and ends its journey. However, this is not the case in the case of real estate. Land, property, and real estate are all terms that I shall refer to as if they are all the same thing throughout this section. Properties described in this manner are just descriptions of the boundaries of the land; no information about any buildings that may be placed on the land is included in this kind of description.

Knowing the exact boundary lines of the land you own is so critical for selecting how you wish to use it only serves to emphasize the need to accurately identify your property when transferring title from one person to another. Both the grantor and the grantee must comprehend exactly what they are selling, giving away, or exchanging. It is also essential that the grantee understand exactly what he or she is getting.

This description of the property is referred to as the legal description of the real estate property in many instances. In general, legal descriptions are constructed using one of three typical ways, which I shall discuss in further detail later in this chapter. For the reason that there may be a few math questions on the exam that are connected to the description of a property, I also go through how to measure elevations for property descriptions and teach you about two different ways that you cannot describe a property.

The next parts will provide three approaches for creating a legal description that may be used everywhere in the United States, as you will see in the following sections. Some sections of the country are indeed more reliant on one system than on another, but this is not universal. Regardless of the state you are in, examiners are eager to know about all three systems you are familiar with. Make no mistake: you do not need to understand just the system of legal description that is most often used in your state; this is a fallacy. No one, even the land surveyor who surveys the property and physically locates its boundaries on the ground in order to generate these legal descriptions, is seeking to turn you into the authorities.

When it comes to passing the test, you must be able to distinguish between the characteristics and significant ideas of each system of legal description, which means you must be able to distinguish between the features and essential concepts of each system of legal description. The metes and bounds technique of legal description explains the limits of a piece of property by identifying the boundaries of the property using specific locations, distances, and compass directions to locate the boundaries of the property. It is common to begin a description from one position and continue it in the same manner for a certain distance, such as following a line or curve in a specific direction to another point. This is known as the place or point of beginning. When the direction changes, the boundary line is drawn out once again in a specific direction and for an exact distance. This is the point at which the direction switches.

Try drawing a rough sketch of this description using a pencil and paper for a little fun. While designing a property like this, it's crucial to remember that the north is up, the south is down, the east is to the right, and the west is to the left when looking at the paper. You'll end up with a square on the page as a result of this. In reality, however, metes and bounds descriptions are seldom as easy as they seem on paper.

According to navigational conventions, the directions are often broken down into degrees, minutes, and seconds, all of which are precise points on a compass, as is typical in the field. When applicable, lengths are measured to the nearest tenth of an inch in certain instances. When defining boundary lines and turning points, turning points are also referred to as natural things, such as rock formations or a stream. In a variety of situations, it may be necessary to use the boundary of another's property as a point of reference. Landowners come and go, rocks move, and streams vanish, yet the landscape remains the same. It is becoming more common to see man-made markings permanently entrenched in the ground replace natural and ownership references. When it comes to turning points, it is often sufficient just to note the beginning or the starting point, rather than documenting each and every one.

The term "monument" refers to any place within the measured bounds that have been identified as being historically important by the surveyors. Monuments, which are sometimes referred to as "turning points in history," maybe either be man-made or natural in their origin. The deed gives a detailed description of the property's boundaries and metes and bounds. In the instance of a large property with a convoluted boundary that includes multiple twists and turns, a metes-and-bounds description might be rather lengthy and detailed. The description may also be used to construct a map, which is referred to as a survey map or just a survey and other documents.

A survey is a process of physically defining the boundaries of property on the ground, which is also known as mapping. In a survey map or sketch, the boundaries of a property are shown or drawn. This portrayal or drawing may or may not include structures that are situated on the property, as well as other information. It is built on a sequence of lines that produce rectangles and squares all throughout the United States, and it is also referred to as "the government survey system." Major meridians (which run north and south) and baselines (which run east and west) are the first two sets of lines, which are referred to as major meridians (which run north and south) and baselines (which run east and west), respectively. Longitude and latitude lines serve as the foundation for the principal meridian and baseline systems in order to establish their respective borders.

If you haven't already forgotten, longitude and latitude are imaginary lines that divide the planet between the north and south poles (longitude) and run parallel to the equator (latitude). It is possible to generate property descriptions based on the intersection points of the primary meridian and baseline lines and their intersection locations (cross each other). In order to define the borders of a piece of property, they are used as a beginning point for the process. The following is a dictionary of terms that may be of assistance:

Quadrangles

Quadrangles (also known as government checks or just checks) are the essential squares of land that make up the rectangular survey system, and they are the building blocks of the rectangular survey system.
They have a surface area of 24 miles square and are bordered by a major meridian as well as a baseline.
The quadrangles, which are further split into 16 townships, encompass an area of about 576 square miles

(more or less) in total. In the United States, townships are six-mile-square segments of a quadrangle that are delineated by township boundaries. Townships are the divisions of a quadrangle that are defined by their size. Townships encompass an area of 36 square miles, give or take a few square miles, and are split into a total of 36 parts. Townships are divided into three types of sections: rural, suburban, and urban.

Sections

Sections of a township are one-mile square and have an area of one square mile, or 640 acres. Townships are divided into sections, which are one-mile square and have an area of 640 acres. Groupings of three sections are used to organize the sections of the book. The United States Geological Survey (USGS) divides sections into quarter sections for the purposes of geological mapping and study. There are many techniques for dividing sections, but the USGS chooses to divide them into quarter sections. Quarter sections, also known as fourth sections, are formed by dividing a section into fourths that are distinguished by their direction from the Center of the section (northwest is NW, northeast is NE, southeast is SE, and southwest is SW) and by the direction from the Center of the section (northwest is NW, northeast is NE, southeast is SE, and southwest is SW) (northeast is NW). The land area of quarter sections is about 160 acres in total. The word "half-section" refers to any two-quarter sections that are next to one another inside a section, and it is often used to refer to the portion in which the two-quarter sections are situated rather than the section itself. Sections that are half the length of a section are normally denoted by a directional notation indicating which half of the section they are placed in. Half-sections have a combined land area of around 320 acres.

Because the earth is curved, lines drawn by the government survey method are only theoretically straight due to the curvature of the earth's axis of rotation. To illustrate the difficulty of drawing straight lines on a rubber ball. Because they start out equal distance apart, as you travel closer to either end of the ball, the lines get closer and closer together until they meet at the Centre. The development of corrective lines and guide meridians was necessary in order to overcome this problem in the government surveying system. Along with every fourth township line, correction lines are found every 24 miles north and south of the baseline and every fourth township line.

The guiding meridians may be located every 24 miles east and west of the major meridian, on each side of the equator. A government check, check, or quadrangle is a rectangular zone that is bordered on two sides by guide meridians and on the other two sides by correction lines, and guide meridians bound that on both sides of the region. Every border of a government checkpoint, checkpoint, or quadrangle is 24 miles long and 24 miles wide, which indicates that each of its boundaries is 24 miles wide.

The size of the United States is represented by a government check, which represents an area of 576 square miles. Be mindful of the fact that, despite the fact that the federal government uses these correction lines and guides meridians to address issues relating to global curvature, they are not the means by which the federal survey system defines land. So, how do the land classification and classification system categories describe it?

Based on the principal meridians and baselines that serve as points of reference for the division, land areas are divided into two kinds of lines: township lines and range lines. Township lines and range lines are the most common forms of lines. Township lines, which run east and west parallel to baselines and divide the land into tiers, are horizontal parallel lines that run east and west parallel to baselines and divide the land into tears. Township lines are horizontal parallel lines that run east and west parallel to baselines and divide the land into tears. Let's consider two lines that are approximately an inch apart and go across this paper from left to right. North and south range lines run parallel to the principal meridian lines in both directions, whereas the range lines go north and south. The intersection of these range lines produces range lines. As an addition to the first two lines, envision two extra lines running up and down the paper, roughly an inch apart from one another, and running up and down the page. You've figured it out; congratulations. Tic Tac Toe is a game that is played aboard. It is possible to make a township by bringing together two range lines and two township lines to create a point of junction between the two lines. It really works like this: this page is filled with lines that flow up and down as well as right and left, resulting in an enormous number of townships to choose from. The township is the main unit of measurement in rectangular surveying.

In a particular area, the intersection of township lines and range lines results in the formation of a total of 16 townships. In a sequential way, the townships are designated by their numerical designations. Assuming that the perimeter of each township is six miles long, a township has a total area of 36 square miles and is defined as having a circumference of six miles. Unlike political subdivisions, townships are not the same thing in this sense. All of the terms used to refer to the final step in the process of creating legal property descriptions, including lot and block system, recorded plat system, recorded map system, lot block tract system, recorded survey system, and filed map system, are synonymous with the process of creating legal property descriptions. In your relicensing course, you will be taught the name that is most often used in your area when applying for a new license. What matters is that the basics remain unchanged.

This strategy is often used in conjunction with a new subdivision or a large piece of property that has been divided into smaller pieces, with the goal of selling or developing each portion on its own merits, as described above. An initial map or plat (they are all the same thing; don't you wish these guys could agree on what to call things?) is created to lay out the boundaries of each (usually numbered) lot or piece of land in order to begin construction on the subdivision.

If a large subdivision is broken into blocks or sections, each of which is then subdivided into lots, it is feasible to divide a large subdivision into smaller subdivisions. It is feasible, for example, to have Lot 2 in Block 1 and Lot 5 in Section A of the same building. The descriptions of the lots' metes and bounds are inscribed on the exterior of each lot. The sole choice accessible to a surveyor is to look at a map and draw the property's boundaries on the actual land, which is the only option available to him. To put it another way, the lot and block system is a hybrid system that makes use of the advantages of another system to its advantage. It is necessary to submit the map to the relevant municipal records office when the survey has been completed. Anyone may submit the map; however, depending on the circumstances, the landowner, an attorney, or a surveyor are most often the ones who do the task for them.

According to the premise, if the map reflected a new subdivision, the development would already have received approval from local zoning, planning, or other government officials. In various states and areas, the records office is called by many different names, but it is generally regarded as a component of the county administration. For the life of the property's existence, the map is filed in the county in which the property is located and is kept on file as a public document on file.

When a document is filed, it is provided to the filer with a record of the filing that includes the filing date and may be marked with a specific reference number that refers to the document, what type of document it is, the book (sometimes referred to as liber, which is Latin for book) in which it is stored, and the page number. If someone is searching for the map at the records office, they will be able to locate it by using this identification number.

Here's everything you need to know

A buyer is looking to buy a lot on Lot 3 in Block 2 of the development I've been talking about. The development is called Mary's Project, which is named after the developer's daughter, who served as the inspiration for the subdivision. An industry-standard real estate sales contract states that the seller must transfer marketable title to the buyer, which means that the title must be free of any reasonable doubts about who the owner is and any faults in the title itself. The purpose of establishing a marketable title is to show that the property's title is free of encumbrances that prohibit it from being sold.

Generally speaking, a cloud on the title is anything that causes the grantor's ownership of the property to be put into doubt. A grantor's ability to establish marketable titles may be demonstrated in a variety of ways, which differ from state to state and even from region to region within the same state. Investigate what is considered normal practice in your state to see whether it matches up. The good news is that, in general, there are a variety of alternate approaches for showing a clear and acceptable title. The following are descriptions of the four most prevalent ways to go about doing things in the modern world:

Abstract of title

Essentially, an abstract of title is a description of what was found during a title search, which involves searching almost all public documents related to the property's title, such as earlier deeds and liens to ascertain whether or not the property is lawfully possessed.

Depending on the state, these papers are often obtained at the county recorder's office or the county's land records office in which the property is situated. Although anyone can search the public records, an abstractor (someone who allows the user to search through title records) or an attorney conducts a title evaluation to find the chain or history of ownership from one owner to the next, looking for gaps in ownership or other factors that show up to cast doubt on the validity of the current owner's claim to the land. An abstractor or an attorney can also conduct a title search on behalf of a client.

Chapter 13: Types of Closing

Buyer and seller are both relieved that they have found the perfect house for their needs, and a closing date has been set for the transaction. What should I do at this point? Following a description of the processes that must be followed before the closure, this chapter discusses the closing process itself and what happens after the closure has taken place. The buyer seeks a house inspection while the seller is preparing to close the deal. While both parties are prepared to close on the property, the lending institution requires an appraisal of the property. It is possible that a problem with one of them may cause the closure to be derailed, or at the very least postponed, completely. In general, closings may be divided into two groups. Traditional closings and escrow closings are two kinds of closings that are governed by the laws of the state in which the property is located.

Traditional closings

This kind of closure, which is also known as the settlement, is popular across most of the United States and is used in many different states. Both the buyer and the seller and their respective attorneys are present during the meeting. Representatives from both the buyer's and seller's financing institutions and a representative from the title insurance firm may participate in the meeting. As a result, the buyer's attorney acts as a fiduciary on behalf of the corporations that are not present at the closing. To receive their commission fees, realtors often attend these events. The ending of the meeting may be done by any of the non-principal participants who are present. Although the buyer's attorney often monitors it, the title company's agent is sometimes in control. In its most basic form, the closing process consists of the signing of documents and the transfer of monies to transfer ownership of the property from the seller to the buyer, as described above. Later in this chapter, we'll discuss how many pieces of paperwork are signed and what kind of papers are signed and what the checks are used for.

Closings of escrow accounts

This kind of closing entails the buyer and seller handing over the documentation that each is responsible for prior to the day of closing to an escrow agent who has been selected by both parties to serve in this capacity. Typically, the person is an attorney, a representative of a title firm, or an agent for an escrow company, among other things. Closing dates are mutually agreed upon by the buyer, seller, and lender, and the principals are obliged to provide all of their completed documentation to the escrow agency by this day. The escrow agency bears closing costs. The contract of sale must be all completed prior to the closing date, and no documentation will be submitted until all terms and conditions have been met, as stated in the contract. The "close of escrow" is the official word used to refer to the actual completion of the transaction. This includes transferring ownership of the property to an escrow service and providing documents from the existing lender confirming that the current mortgage has been paid off. For example, the seller must provide documents indicating that his or her title to the property is free of encumbrances, which may compel him or her to take further measures. During the closing process, the buyer must present the escrow agent with a certified check for the purchase price and any papers related to the new mortgage loan. Also required is paperwork demonstrating that the buyer has obtained all of the required insurance coverage for the property. Before a transaction may be completed, a variety of legal documents must be collected. Some of these are the responsibility of the vendor, while others are the duty of the buyer.

Documents for the closing

The seller is obliged to offer a marketable title to the property, which is the most crucial document that he or she must supply. In order for the transaction to be completed, the seller must produce documents demonstrating that they have the right to transfer the title and that the title is free and clear of encumbrances. It is possible to do this by one of four methods: In the real estate industry, an abstract of title is a report that details the ownership and transfer of a piece of real estate. It may be obtained by doing a title search on the property in question. In most cases, the buyer's attorney will analyze the report, and if the attorney concludes that the title is in good standing, the attorney will issue what is known as an attorney's opinion of title. It does not mean that the buyer is the legal owner of the property. When it comes to real estate, a certificate of title is an expert-written opinion supplied by a title company or an attorney about a piece of property's ownership and legal status.

It is obtained in the same manner as an abstract of title is obtained: by conducting a search of public records, and it does not indicate ownership of the property in any way whatsoever. Purchasers of real estate are protected against future claims against the property by third parties who get title insurance before they close on the purchase. For the purpose of protecting his or her (the buyer's) investment in the property, the buyer purchases title insurance, which is often financed by the lender and paid for by the borrower. Title insurance protects both the borrower and the lender. Obtaining a title insurance coverage is possible after a deed of conveyance or certificate of title has been issued, or it may be acquired after a title search has been conducted on the property in question, depending on the circumstances.

Certificate of Torrens

More than a dozen states have adopted the Torrens System, which is a land title registration system that the state government insures. All land titles are maintained on file by the state in a register, also known as a record, where they are easily accessible. Once the sale is completed, the buyer must get a certificate of Torrens title from the county registrar in the county where the property is located before completing the transfer of title. Following a careful investigation of all necessary documents, the court orders that the registration record be modified to reflect the new ownership and that a certificate be provided to the newly acquired property.

It is impossible to revoke or cancel the ownership of the title or property if the title is indefeasible, which indicates that no one has the jurisdiction to do so. During the selling process, the seller removes liens and other encumbrances that have a negative impact on the title, resulting in a marketable title being formed. It is a lien on the property's title that is typically paid off with the proceeds of the sale at the time of the transaction's completion date. Liens may be obtained for a variety of reasons, including unpaid taxes. The seller may be able to pay off these debts from the proceeds of the sale at the time of closing, or even before closing if he or she is able to do so before the closing. In addition to liens, other types of encumbrances, such as easements and deed limits, may be recorded against a property's title.

During the title search, any concerns that are uncovered by the buyer and his or her attorney are investigated and must be resolved with the seller prior to closing. Some easements and limits "run with the property," and the lender's title policy will stipulate that if the easement or restriction is not removed, the lender will not be liable for any loss of title. According to the National Association of Realtors, customers are often ready to acquire property with easements if the easement will not interfere with their use of the land and if the easement will not degrade the marketability of the property's ownership title. Deeds are written legal documents that convey and act as documentation of a person's legal right to possess a particular piece of real land.

They are often used in the field of real estate.

For the title to be transferred, a new deed must be transferred from the seller to the buyer during the closing process, which takes place during the closing process. The deed and mortgage will be recorded, and the lender will get the recorded mortgage as well as the note in return for the money they have loaned to the buyer. The registered deed and a copy of the recorded mortgage will be sent to the buyer for their records. Several thousand dollars in expenses are expected and planned for as a result of the shutdown. According to HUD guidelines, a buyer of a house that is being purchased with an FHA-insured loan has the right to inspect the closing expenses one day before the closing date in most instances.

On the statement of closing expenditures, some money will be displayed as credits to the seller or the buyer, and certain money will be shown as debits to the seller or the buyer on the statement of closing expenses, respectively. It is also feasible to prorate revenue and expenditures prior to crediting or debiting them in the accounting system. Even after the paperwork has been completed and the keys have been turned over to the buyer by the seller, there is still work to be done. What needs to be done is to complete the following responsibilities: The final closing statement is prepared by one of the attorneys or by the title company on behalf of the client and is signed by both parties.

This transaction will be legitimate only if all of the necessary documents are submitted with the appropriate county office, which serves as a constructive notice to the general public that the transaction has taken place. In order to complete the transaction, it is essential to pay the recording costs and transfer tax, if any are relevant. Depending on the circumstances, some sellers may also be required to file Form 1099-S when filing their personal income tax returns for the tax year in which they made the transaction.

Individuals who sell a residential property for less than $250,000 or a couple who sells a residential property for less than $500,000 are excluded from the restriction. Generally speaking, there are two types of closings that are employed in the United States: the normal closing and the escrow closing. To complete their deal, a seller must provide a marketable title at closing, demonstrating that they have the authority to transfer ownership. The title is free and clear of any liens or encumbrances, among other things. In order to acquire a marketable title, it is essential to get one of the following documents: an abstract of title, a certificate of title, title insurance, or a certificate of Torrens. Following the completion of the transaction, the buyer is given a new deed from the seller.

Similarly, it is necessary for the buyer to arrive at the closing with the mortgage financing in hand and prepared to pay the other costs that are typically assigned to buyers, while it is necessary for the seller to arrive at the closing with a marketable title and prepared to pay the costs that are typically assigned to sellers. Depending on the circumstances, certain expenses and revenues are divided between the seller and the buyer on a prorated basis. Purchase and sale payments to the buyer and seller are recorded on the closing statement as credits or debits, accordingly. An end-of-closure statement is generated, the mortgage and deed are registered, the recording and transfer expenses are paid, and the loan is discharged upon the completion of the closing.

Chapter 14: Taxes and Monetary Assessment

Taxes are an essential source of revenue for all levels of government since they fund the majority of its activities. Rather than state or federal taxes, which are assessed at the state or federal level, property taxes are charged at the local level and have an influence on real estate. When you submit your federal income tax return, you will be entitled to deduct your property taxes (as well as any state income taxes) from your total income. Among other things, local governments use property tax money to pay for a number of services, including employee compensation, basic road and bridge upkeep, and equipment and supplies for police and fire agencies, among other things. School and bridge construction and other large-scale infrastructure projects are funded via the issue of bonds to investors, with the dividends paid out using tax money collected from individuals who invest. Taxation authority over its citizens is shared by municipal governments, such as towns, cities, and counties, sometimes known as special districts or special-purpose districts.

Depending on the state, special-purpose districts may include school districts, water and sewer districts, irrigation districts, and metropolitan transportation agencies, among other things. In order to function, they must raise revenue through taxes, which are included in the property tax bills that are collected by the municipality in which they operate. Following that, the tax revenue is distributed to the special districts in line with the tax rates established by the special districts.

In the case of a property tax payment for real estate assessed at $256,000, the portion of the payment that is paid by an irrigation district may be as much as $154. Governments don't borrow money to fund recurring operating costs such as salaries and benefits; instead, they borrow money to cover large, one-time expenses such as the purchase of open land for a public park. In order to finance their operations, they must first develop a budget, which is then followed by a decision of how they will pay for the goods contained in that budget. If the tax revenue does not cover the whole amount of expenditures on the budget, the municipality will be compelled to make budgetary cuts to balance the books. Alternatively, if the savings are inadequate, the municipality may elect to increase property taxes to make up the difference. In the case of property taxes, they are referred to as ad valorem taxes, which implies that they are computed on the basis of the value of the property subject to tax. Alternatively, the value may be stated as a rate of mills per dollar (for example, 50 mills for $1), with a mill equaling one-tenth of a penny. It is also possible to calculate the value using a specific tax amount per $100 or $1,000 of assessed value (for example, $3 per $100 written as $3/$100, or $30 per $1,000 written as $30/$1,000). A specific tax amount per $100 or $1,000 of assessed value (for example, $3 per $100 written as $3/$100, or $30 per $1,000 written as $30/$1,000) is also possible. State tax requirements specify that a municipality must have all of the property within its jurisdiction appraised every few years, and that this must be done by a certified appraiser. This treatment is performed on average once every 10 years, according to industry standards. It is possible that the act of enhancing a property, such as by constructing a garage, or the act of selling a property will both trigger appraisals.

Depending on whether the whole town is being reviewed at the same time, the appraisals may be carried out by the local tax assessor's department, or an outside firm may be hired to do the task on a contract basis. All of the properties in the municipality are appraised by the appraisers, who walk about taking notes and taking measures, and then write up what they have discovered.

When calculating the value of each property based on the information they have acquired, they employ standard tables that assessors use to make their calculations. When determining the property tax for a particular property, the tax assessor applies a formula (millage or unit of taxes per $100 of assessed value) to the property's assessed value and calculates the property tax for the next fiscal year. Regardless of whether or not a tax assessment is being done in a given year, the tax assessor is responsible for doing this task on a year-round basis. It is necessary to review the tax rate on an annual basis since the municipal budget fluctuates on an annual basis as a result of increases or decreases in anticipated demand, increases or decreases in inflation, among other variables. A tax bill in the mail, detailing the amount of property taxes a homeowner must pay for the next year, is received by every homeowner every year. Depending on the conditions, the assessed value of real estate may or may not be an accurate predictor of the property's current market value. If an extremely unusual event occurs, the value of a house between tax assessments may be negatively affected. When the economy was in a slump in 2007-09, for example, a precipitous decrease in property values as possible, as was the case in various parts of the country when house prices plummeted from week to week. It is more usual for market values to rise above or fall below a property's assessed value when tax assessments are only performed every 10 years. The value of real estate in a certain township may increase as a consequence of the construction of a new firm in the area, which will result in the creation of a significant number of new jobs and employees for the community. When a firm goes out of business, it is possible that property values may decline as a consequence of the closure. Furthermore, suppose no alterations have been made to a property for an extended period of time. In that case, the residence's assessed value may be much lower than the market value by the end of the 10-year period. Municipalities have the ability to assess real estate at its full market value, regardless of where it is located. If an owner fails to pay the special assessment due, the board has the authority to penalize them and even place a lien on their property. Purchasing into an association, cooperative, or condo that has a current assessment will result in the buyer being liable for those payments as we advance unless the buyer negotiates with the seller to have those payments covered by the buyer at the time of purchase. According to the law, prospective buyers should be informed of an assessment by both the seller and the real estate agent. When fees are paid to a government entity, they are seen as taxation.

It is common for the seller to be liable for paying a transfer fee, sometimes known as a transfer tax, to the county when transferring ownership of a piece of real land from the seller to the buyer during the course of a real estate transaction. In addition, the buyer is responsible for paying a recording fee to the county at the time of the transaction. This price includes all of the documents required to register the transfer of ownership from the seller to the buyer into the public record, record the new mortgage, cancel the previous mortgage of record, and record the satisfaction of the loan. This price covers the entire transaction, including all of the documents required to register the transfer of ownership from the seller to the buyer into the public record, record the new mortgage, cancel the previous mortgage of record, and record a satisfaction of loan. When calculating closing expenditures, it is included in the Good Faith Estimate for closing costs and is included in the final closing statement. Despite the buyer being accountable for this tax, it is often charged to the seller. It is possible that the bylaws of co-ops require the payment of a flip tax when a unit is sold in some places where they are popular, such as New York City, while in other circumstances, the flip tax may be disregarded completely. The regulations provide that if the rules are followed properly, one of the parties is accountable for the payment of the amount in issue. Even though it is referred to as "flip tax," it is not a tax in the traditional sense. An option to purchase or sell a cooperative unit is contingent on the cooperative receiving a monetary payment from a member. When it comes to the co-op, it's a way to raise money without increasing the monthly co-op charges.

Chapter 15: 7 Study Tips for Passing Your Real Estate Exam

Passing your real estate test is the first step in launching your profession. If you are like a few of our students, this might be frightening, particularly if you've been out of school for a long time. This does not have to be the case. What matters is that you comprehend the knowledge required to pass the real estate examination. Consider the following study tips to alleviate some of your frustration and increase your chances of success.

Review What Will Be on the Exam?

Spend a few minutes reviewing the material covered in the actual real estate test. If you were one of our students. Simply having a rudimentary idea of what is on the test helps alleviate many students' worries. The state gives a percentage breakdown of the subjects covered on the exam. This ensures that there are no unpleasant shocks on exam day.

Make digital or physical notes on important concepts.

Consider producing notecards or flashcards with central themes as you review your notes from your pre-license study. Create them in the form of a question with the answer on the back. Flashcard applications are also available if you wish to learn on your phone. Additionally, it has been demonstrated that the act of physiologically writing things down can aid in memory retention.

Examine Your Notes

If you haven't already, read over all of your resources. Make a list of pertinent subjects for your real estate test. It's a good idea to keep track of anything you're uncertain about or really specialized aspects, such as vocabulary phrases or other general real estate ideas. As you go, keep in mind how critical it is to preserve this knowledge. It's not only for the test; it's also relevant to day-to-day agent jobs. For instance, if a subject is unfamiliar to you, search for a real-world example of how it applies to your job or the work you perform. This way, you'll have a better idea of what to anticipate

Don't Contact Practicing Agents

I would avoid lengthy discussions with other real estate brokers. Typically, they will remark something along the lines of "Don't worry about what's on the real estate test; you won't need any of it anyhow." The continuous reminders of how scholarly and impractical the ideas assessed are might actually deter some of our pupils from planning and studying adequately. While it is true that the real estate test covers a vast range of subjects, not all of which are pertinent to every transaction, it is critical to maintain a laser-like concentration on the end objective of passing the real estate exam. If you're unable to refrain, speak with agents who can assist you in making critical judgments and learning how to negotiate tough issues. These agents may provide context for the information you're studying. Additionally, they may help you relax.

Take a Few Real Estate Practice Exams

It is critical that you have access to state-specific real estate licensing practice examinations. Fortunately for you, our system is contemporary and up to date, ensuring that they reflect the most recent changes to the real estate exam. Concentrating on our real estate practice examinations might help you identify areas where you can improve your study skills. Avoid taking them consecutively. Rather than that, utilize them while you study to determine which topics you should concentrate on coming ahead.

Learn How to Take Tests

While knowing the content required to pass the real estate licensing exam is vital, it's also beneficial to have some test-taking skills, particularly if you haven't lately dealt with high-pressure assessments. Consider the following tactics: Each question should be read carefully. Occasionally, you will omit phrases such as "if" or "all" - which will alter the result. Avoid rushing during the examination. Take your time reading the data and analyzing it strategically. Continue to breathe during your examination. If you feel yourself swamped or under excessive strain, now is the time to shut your eyes, take a deep breath in, and slow your pulse rate. Ensure that you get enough sleep in the week before the test. Avoid binging the night before, since this might impair your cognitive ability later in the day. Attend your exam on time. Get a solid sense of the area's layout. You want to be at ease. If you do not immediately know the solution to a question, skip it. You may always return to it later. Avoid devoting an excessive amount of time to a single question. Avoid rushing during the examination. Take your time and concentrate. If you're having significant difficulty with test-taking, conduct a few practice examinations in a formal setting, such as a library or office area. This may assist in providing you with some peace of mind.

Maintain a positive and upbeat attitude

Passing your real estate exam is a step towards starting a new career. It is a lot of work – and that can seem like a big mountain to climb. However, focus on the big picture. This is a career that you are going to love. The more hands-on experience you have, the better your outcome will be. Practicing for your real estate exam can be a very eye-opening experience. This is what you'll soon be an expert in, helping others achieve their property ownership goals.

Practice Test 1

Question Number	Question	Answer
1	Maxwell Real Estate agent Jan Pearson is assisting Mary Fitz in her search for a townhouse. The residence was advertised by Roy Alexander, who works for the same company as the seller. Is it possible to guarantee that there is no confusion about who Maxwell Real Estate is representing, and what kind of agency offers the most protection for both the seller and Jan Pearson? (A) Buyer agency (B) Designated agency (C) Dual agency (D) Alternate agency	A
2	Harvey McDonald has just relocated to a townhouse that is separated from its neighbor by a thin strip of land in the front. For the last 20 years, the neighbor has been growing flowers on this stretch. In response, the neighbor tells him that the property is hers and that she wants to continue planting on it, regardless of what his deed says about it. She is claiming ownership of the land. (A) as a party wall. (B) by adverse possession. (C) by inverse condemnation. (D) by voluntary alienation.	B
3	Between Louise Parkhurst's three property lots, which she owns, there is at least one common boundary that they share. In the first place, there are three distinct forms to consider. Unlike the square, the triangle has a front that is 90' and a depth that is 210', while the triangle only has one side that is 210'. There are two rectangles with front measurements of 170' and depth measurements of 210' in the second and third forms, and a rectangle with front measurements of 170' and depth measurements in the fourth shape. What is the total land size of the three properties in terms of square footage? (A) 1.50 acres (B) 1.75 acres (C) 2.25 acre (D) 2.05 acres	B
4	As a result of Jenifer James' FHA-insured mortgage, he is required to purchase a insurance coverage. (A) conventional mortgage. (B) conforming mortgage	D

	(C) nonconforming mortgage. (D) fixed-rate mortgage. (E) insurance coverage	
5	In the City and County of Philadelphia, real estate transactions are subject to a transfer tax. Is it possible to calculate the effective tax rate on $444,000 if the transfer tax is $8,880, based on a $1,000 investment? (A) 0.02 percent (B) 0.2 percent (C) 2 percent (D) 20 percent	B
6	Which of the following characteristics is considered "personality" in the context of a real estate transaction? (A) Breakfast nook (B) Refrigerator (C) Dishwasher (D) Chandelier	A
7	In which of the following situations does the seller's account get a debit at the moment of settlement? (A) Earnest money (B) Survey cost (C) Property tax payment (D) Prepayment penalty	B
8	According to the following assumptions, what is the amount due to the seller at closing on prepaid taxes if it is determined as follows: a selling price of $765,832, an assessment rate of 65 percent, and a tax rate of 32 mills; a closure date of July 1, and the seller has paid the taxes in advance. (A) $632.22 (B) $1,327.44 (C) $7,964.65 (D) $15,929.30	D
9	Rochelle Michael will purchase the leather couch and chairs that are already in the living room of the Dubinsky's house after closing on the purchase. In addition to her monthly mortgage payment, she also has a monthly furnishings payment. She will be presented with a prize or awards. (A) open mortgage. (B) blanket mortgage. (C) package mortgage. (D) wraparound mortgage.	C
10	The bigger the quantity of land in a certain location that has been set aside for a specific purpose, the better... (A) results in a lower value for the land than if there were less land zoned for that use. (B) has no effect on the value of the land. (C) drives up the value of the land.	C

	(D) affects the value negatively or positively depending on the zoned use.	
11	All of the foregoing expenses, with the exception of the fees, would be itemized in the case of a borrower who obtains an MLDS. (A) real estate commission. (B) appraisal fee. (C) life insurance. (D) credit report.	A
12	One of the most expensive real estate transactions in history takes place on July 5, when a property with a rental cottage sells for $275,000. What is the best way to figure out who owes what to whom if rent is due on the fifth of the month? (A) Not enough information (B) Buyer owes (C) Seller owes (D) Neither owes	C
13	On their new house, the Taylors will be covered by a general warranty. They anticipate that it will include all of the following WITH THE EXCEPTION OF (A) covenant of right to convey. (B) covenant of right to grant. (C) covenant of quiet enjoyment. (D) covenant against encumbrances	B
14	For the last 93 years, the Doyle family has held coastal property. In that time, the ocean has slowly but gradually encroached on the beach in front of their home, until it is now just 10 feet from the entrance of their home. This procedure is referred to as (A) alienation. (B) propulsion. (C) erosion. (D) accretion.	C
15	In addition to a home, Charlie Samuels was the owner of various plots of property. He died without leaving a will, although he was survived by three daughters. Which of the following statements is correct in this situation? (A) The government takes the property by escheat. (B) The government takes the property by right of eminent domain. (C) The daughters claim testamentary trust. (D) The daughters claim title by descent.	D
16	It is very likely that the appraiser will utilize the following criteria when evaluating a townhouse that is being purchased for rental purposes: (A) cost approach. (B) sales comparison approach.	D

	(C) reproduction and replacement approach. (D) income approach.	
17	Those who get an FHA-insured loan must pay an upfront insurance payment that is equal to what percentage of the loan's value? (A) 1.75 percent (B) 2 percent (C) 2.25 percent (D) 3 percent	C
18	Jumbo mortgages are loans that are larger than the average home loan... (A) are mortgages that permit the mortgager to borrow additional money so that the mortgage can increase back to its original amount. (B) are above the limit on mortgages for securitization on the secondary mortgage market. (C) include senior and junior mortgages. (D) are the same as a 30-year, fixed-rate interest-only mortgage.	B
19	If a home depreciates at a rate of 3.75 percent per year for four years and was once worth $132,800, how much is it now worth in today's dollars? (A) $106,420 (B) $110,870 (C) $112,880 (D) $157,720	C
20	In a real estate transaction, the grantor is the legal word for the buyer who? (A) buyer. (B) seller. (C) lending institution for the buyer. (D) lending institution for the seller.	B
21	Nonconforming usage may be shown by the use of which of the following examples: (A) A convenience store in a commercial zone (B) A bar and restaurant in a residential zone (C) A gas station that predates garden apartments in the neighborhood (D) An elementary school in a mixed-use zone	C
22	A 139,392 square foot lot in a development would sell for $45,675 per acre if the property is valued at $45,675 per acre. (A) $146,160 (B) $156,160 (C) $166,160 (D) $176,160	A

23	It has been recommended to the Johnsons by their attorney that they get a thorough history of the property that they are planning to purchase. They must place an order for a/an (A) certificate of title (B) abstract of title. (C) Torrens certificate. (D) title company's opinion of title.	B
24	Joe Sanders has fallen behind on his mortgage payments, and the First National Mortgage Company has filed a lawsuit in order to get an order allowing the company to sell Sanders' property. What type of foreclosure is this, , and why is it happening? (A) Judicial foreclosure (B) Strict foreclosure (C) Default foreclosure (D) No judicial foreclosure	B
25	If the property in the above example sells for less than the mortgage balance, First National may petition the court for a/an injunction to prevent the sale from proceeding... (A) deficiency judgment (B) default judgment. (C) short sale judgment. (D) underwater mortgage judgment.	A
26	All of the following are restrictive covenants that are often seen in sub development deeds and are described in detail below. EXCEPT (A) schedule for trash pickup. (B) limitations on the number of pets. (C) rules regarding the rental of a property. (D) regulations regarding the setbacks of homes.	A
27	Lamont Johns completed the sale of a home for $452,850. How much money did the seller get from the transaction after closing fees of $1,800 and Davis's 5.63 percent commission were taken into consideration? (A) $422,520.45 (B) $423,720.45 (C) $424,320.45 (D) $425,620.45	C
28	If any insect issues were detected in the house, the Millers inserted a condition into the contract of sale that said that the seller would address them before closing. During the examination, it was revealed that there were Carpenter ants. A walk-through revealed that the vendor had failed to resolve the problem. The Millers are capable of performing all of the responsibilities listed below. EXCEPT (A) walk away from the deal if this is a contingency of sale. (B) go through with the closing and take the house as-is.	C

	(C) go through with the closing, but force the seller to pay for the remediation out of the proceeds of the sale. (D) postpone the closing for 5 days while the seller remediates the problem.	
29	2,500 square feet, three bedrooms, and three and a half baths are on the market thanks to Randy Lamont. He will undertake which market analysis in order to calculate a sales price? . (A) sales comparison analysis. (B) comparative market analysis. (C) highest and best use analysis. (D) site valuation.	B
30	A Lis pendent is a public notification that a case is currently underway in a court of law... (A) between tenants. (B) between a divorcing couple. (C) involving a lien on property. (D) by the owner of a property against the property manager.	C
31	Oliver James and Lamont Davis are joint owners of a number of residential homes in the Los Angeles area. When Jack dies away, Kirby becomes the only owner and operator of the firm. Which of the following sorts of ownership relationships must have existed between the two parties in order for this to have happened? (A) Tenancy in common (B) Joint tenancy (C) Partnership (D) Corporation	B
32	The need that listing agreements be in writing is mandated by the government... (A) a state's real estate licensing laws. (B) a state's Statute of Frauds. (C) RESPA. (D) HUD.	A
33	The fiduciary responsibility of reasonable skill and diligence refers to an agent's obligation to use reasonable care and diligence in the performance of his or her duties.... (A) alert prospective buyers to the presence of small animals so they aren't accidentally let out during a showing. (B) be careful not to damage anything when showing a house. (C) market a property accurately. (D) check with other agents about possible showings before arranging to take their buyers to a house.	C

| 34 | The real valuation of a home with a $4,485 tax bill is calculated using the following assumptions: the tax rate is $0.45 per hundred and the rate of assessment is 67 percent.
(A) $1,023,473.54
(B) $1,085,555.56
(C) $1,620,232.18
(D) $1,852,893.53 | C |
| 35 | Mary Jane Turo is a 60-year-old African-American lady who is parenting her ten-year-old grandson. She is a single mother. She submits an application to the Lakefront Apartment complex in order to rent an apartment. Under all of the above categories, she is protected. EXCEPT
(A) familial status.
(B) race.
(C) gender.
(D) age. | D |

36	It is possible that the Lucas family may purchase a riverfront property on the Mississippi River. It has been explained to them by their realtor that they would enjoy riparian rights. According to which of the following definitions would the realtor opt for? (A) They will own from the water's edge to 200 feet out into the river. (B) They will own to the water's edge or to the average or the mean high-water mark. (C) They will own from the water's edge to the center of the waterway. (D) They will own from the water's edge to the ship channel wherever it begins.	B
37	The term "easement in gross" refers to which of the following? (A) Sewer line (B) Neighborhood child's cutting through your backyard to get to the bus stop though you have asked the parents to stop the child (C) Driveway through your side yard for a neighbor who has no other access to the street (D) Court-ordered right of way for a footpath through your beachfront property	A
38	A typical mortgage note comprises the following information: (A) amount of the mortgage, interest rate, and schedule of payments. (B) schedule of payments, habendum, and acceleration clause. (C) acceleration clause, interest rate, and prepayment clause.	A

	(D) property tax rate, interest rate, and schedule of payments.	
39	In the following advertisement, which sentence would be deemed a violation of the Fair Housing Act? *"Two-bedroom apartment for rent in elevator building with handicap-accessible bathroom"? Preferably, a husband and wife. Welcome to the party, kids!"* (A) "Elevator building" (B) "Handicap-accessible bathroom" (C) "Husband and wife preferred" (D) "Children welcome"	C
40	When you have a loan with an interest rate of 5.57 percent and a monthly interest payment of $763.98, what is the principal amount owed? (A) $176,987.32 (B) $164,591.74 (C) $154,982.53 (D) $142,583.62	B
41	The Oliver's are in the process of purchasing their first house. The actual ownership of the house will be transferred to them after the transaction is completed and (A) deed is recorded in the appropriate recording office. (B) deed is delivered to the Oliver's at the closing. (C) notary notarizes the deed. (D) Oliver's hand over the check to the person conducting the closing.	B
42	The Oliver's have made a check for property taxes to be put in an escrow account. This is presented at the closing as a (A) credit to the seller. (B) debit to the seller. (C) credit to the buyer. (D) debit to the buyer	D
43	All of the words listed below are trigger terms that demand complete disclosure in mortgage advertisements. EXCEPT (A) amount of a down payment. (B) dollar amount of finance charges. (C) term of the mortgage. (D) APR.	D
44	A desk is rented and all of Charlie James' expenditures, including promoting the homes that he lists, are covered by his own funds. On all of his sales, he earns a 100 percent commission. Charlie is a\an ~~actor.~~ (A) franchiser. (B) independent contractor. (C) licensee. (D) employee of a brokerage.	B

45	A fire insurance policy has 4 months and 16 days remaining on its expiration date. What is the monetary value of the unused part of an insurance that cost $272 for three years? (A) $27.43 (B) $34.24 (C) $102.84 (D) $94.67	B
46	Following a closure, it is necessary to record the proper documentation. (A) closure. (B) constructive notice. (C) actual notice. (D) express notice.	B
47	Harold and Janelle Scott want to purchase a property in a neighborhood that is close to public transportation, such as the subway and bus networks. Which of the following factors has an impact on house values? (A) Economic factor (B) Environmental factor (C) Political factor (D) Social factor	B
48	When an appraiser is evaluating the quality of interior finishes, he or she will consider all of the factors listed below WITH the exception of (A) countertops. (B) walls. (C) HVAC. (D) presence or absence of molding.	C
49		B
50		B

Practice Test 2

Question Number	Question	Answer
1	Which of the following best describes pottage in its most true form? (A) The process of acquiring land (B) Increase in the value of individual lots when combined (C) Another name for the lots in a planned unit development (D) The division of land in a rectangular survey system	B
2	In relation to pottage, which of the following assertions is the most accurate? (A) Annual cap on the interest rate (B) Life of loan interest rate cap (C) Payment cap (D) Index cap	D
3	In front of the Mason Company's apartment complex, the Jansen Outdoor Display Company plans to install a billboard on the roof, which would be visible from I-95. The Jansen Company contacts the Mason Company in order to secure a key that will allow them access to the roof. (A) lease allowing it to erect a billboard. (B) tenancy in common of the rooftop. (C) syndication. (D) sublease on the roof.	A
4	The Mason Company denies the Jansen Company's request due to a provision in the deed that it received when it purchased the property from Tracy James. The Mason Company bases its decision on this provision. If the Mason Company agrees to the Jansen Company's proposition, it will forfeit its ownership of the land. In order for the clause to be effective, it must have transmitted some type of ownership. (A) Leasehold with conditions (B) Qualified fee conditional ownership (C) Estate at will (D) Estate with qualifications	B
5	Agent Jeff Jackson gets a commission of $7,488 on the sale of a home on Cherry Street in New York City. In the event that he was contracted to receive 45 percent of the fee on a transaction for $256,000, what was the total commission rate? (A) 0.016 (B) 0.029 (C) 0.065 (D) 0.075	C

6	When the 2009–10 homebuyers' tax credit was extended, it created an environment in which buyers were racing to close while the incentive was still in effect. This resulted in a flurry of sales activity as a result of what economic factor? (A) Change (B) Highest and best use (C) Competition (D) Externalities	A
7	The word "discharge" refers to the process through which a principal discharges a real estate agent... (A) revocation. (B) renunciation. (C) reversion. (D) release.	A
8	In a review, an elevator that is old would be graded as a/an (A) curable physical deterioration. (B) curable economic obsolescence. (C) incurable functional obsolescence. (D) curable functional obsolescence.	A
9	Property owners who have littoral rights are entitled to all of the benefits listed below. EXCEPT (A) to build a dock out into the water from their land. (B) to launch a boat into the water from their land. (C) to maintain an inland no-trespassing zone beginning at the high tide water mark. (D) to refuse others the use of their shoreline to ground or launch boats.	D
10	Thanks to a savings and loan, the Fong's are able to get a 90 percent loan on the assessed value of $265,900. What is the interest rate on the loan if the interest payment for the first month is $1,046.98 dollars? (A) 3.22% (B) 4.37% (C) 5.25% (D) 6.87%	C
11	Before a construction permit may be utilized, it must first be granted by the appropriate authority... (A) review by the zoning board. (B) zoning variance. (C) review by the planning board. (D) review by the municipal building department or similar department.	D
12	Mortgage lenders are required to terminate PMI coverage on mortgages after the mortgagor has paid the amount down to zero. (A) 80 percent. (B) 78 percent. (C) 75 percent. (D) 72 percent	B

13	Which of the following acts is prohibited under antitrust laws? A) A developer building four PUDs in a single city (B) Four real estate brokers deciding on the customary rate for sales commissions in their city (C) Four brokers sharing the costs of highway billboards advertising the benefits of living in their city (D) A mortgage broker offering the same interest rate on construction loans to two different developers	B
14	Which of the following is a provision of the Real Estate Settlement Procedures Act? (A) A certain amount of money equal to 6 months of taxes and insurance must be held in an escrow account. (B) Lenders must pay interest on the money held in mortgages escrow accounts . (C) A lender may be required to take out PMI on a borrower's mortgage, depending on the down payment. (D) The lender must tell borrowers why their loan has been turned down.	D
15	Selma McMullen owns the unoccupied ground close to her home, which she uses for gardening. This item is valued at $45,000, whilst her home is valued at $135,000. In the event that both are assessed at 85 percent of their value and taxed at a rate of 6.3 dollars per thousand for schools, 4.2 dollars per thousand for the county, and 2.2 dollars per thousand for the municipality, what is her monthly tax bill? (A) $9,693.90 (B) $1,943.10 (C) $642.60 (D) $336.60	B
16	When a $120,000 property is assessed at 55% of its market value and taxed at $3.20 per $100 of market value, how much money do you owe in property taxes? (A) $211.20 (B) $2,112 (C) $3,840 (D) $384	B
17	A recent sale of a 52,000-square-foot office building brought $972,800 in revenue. What is the predicted rate of return if the monthly revenue is $0.375 per square foot and the rate of return is 12%? (A) 2.4% (B) 24% (C) 2% (D) 20%	B
18	A recent sale of a 52,000-square-foot office building brought $972,800 in revenue. What is the predicted rate of return if the	A

	monthly revenue is $0.375 per square foot and the rate of return is 12%? (A) SARA (B) CERCLA (C) Brownfields Program (D) LUST Trust Fund	
19	On a home loan disclosure statement, you may view a list of the expenses that were incurred. That list is made of... (A) loan amount, notary, disability insurance. (B) deed preparation, fire insurance, loan amount. (C) appraisal, disability insurance, deed preparation. (D) fire insurance, loan amount, title insurance. practice test	D
20	The Liam's are working hard to complete the construction of their new home. They are paying using a four-point discount on their credit card. In what way does it benefit you to pay discount points? (A) Paying points reduces the mortgage. (B) Paying points reduces the interest rate on the mortgage. (C) Paying points reduces the sales price of the property. (D) Paying points reduces the overall closing costs for the buyer.	B
21	Bill Clyde's home is purchased by Keisha Erwin for $376,875. He filled the 200-gallon oil tank on the first of February. In the tank when he sold the home on May 15th, there were 127 gallons of water left in it. In the event that Keisha wastes gasoline that costs $3.15 per gallon, how much does she repay Bill for the oil she has wasted? (A) $229.95 (B) $342.87 (C) $400.05 (D) $0.00	C
22	Noah James has taken the choice to invest in real estate by purchasing a condominium. Which of the following institutions would be ready to provide him a loan to help him out financially? (A) Mortgage broker (B) Ginner Mae (C) FHA (D) Credit union	D
23	The appraisers classify items such as bathroom fixtures, countertops, and floors as belonging to the category of personal property... (A) physical details. (B) environmental factors. (C) finishes. (D) interior design.	C
24	Private covenants put on the deeds of a subdivision are enforceable in the courts of law. (A) federal law only. (B) federal and state law.	D

	(C) municipal governments only.	
	(D) homeowner associations only.	
25	The neighborhood Mini Mart was sold for $1,280,000, which included a 7% commission fee, according to the sale contract. Is it possible to calculate the percentage of commission if the seller's broker earned $51,072? (A) 0.57 (B) 0.67 (C) 0.77 (D) 0.87	A
26	William is now working on a URAR utilizing the cost-based approach. He is responsible for filling out all of the following things. EXCEPT (A) estimated site value. (B) gross adjustments. (C) total depreciation. (D) value of site improvements.	B
27	On August 10, a townhouse went under the hammer for $123,000. From March 1 to February 28, taxes totaling $3,760.90 were due and paid in full on March 1, for the tax year that ran from March 1 to February 28. The $189 monthly association fees were due and payable in full on August 1, and they were received in full. What, if any, money is owed, and to whom does it owe it? (A) $2,215.40 to the buyer (B) $2,215.40 to the seller (C) $2,089.40 to the buyer (D) $2,089.40 to the seller	B
28	The Davidsons are considering purchasing a cooperative. At the completion of the course, they will get a certificate... (A) ground lease. (B) joint tenancy lease. (C) tenancy in common lease. (D) proprietary lease.	D
29	The term "open listing" refers to which of the following? (A) Seller and agent sign an agreement that the agent will get whatever is the difference between the seller's desired price and the actual price. (B) The agent acts as an intermediary between seller and buyers. (C) The agent represents both the seller and the buyer. (D) The seller releases a listing to mule- tiple realtors.	D
30	The Residential Lead-Based Paint Hazard Reduction Act of 1978 forbids the use of lead-based paint in residential buildings, including residences. (A) the seller must have the property, if constructed before 1978, inspected for lead paint before putting the property on the market.	D

	(B) neither the seller's nor buyer's agent has a responsibility to tell the buyer about the possible presence of lead paint in a house that was constructed prior to 1978. (C) the seller must remediate any lead paint before selling a property built before 1978. (D) the seller must inform the buyer of the existence of lead paint on the property.	
31	The Williamses are in the process of purchasing a condominium. All of the following are prevalent regions of ownership in the United States. EXCEPT (A) lobby. (B) fitness gym. (C) rooftop sun deck. (D) storage cage.	D
32	Which of the following is normally deducted from the buyer's account when a property is purchased? (A) Cost of the title insurance (B) Taxes paid to the time of the closing (C) Deed preparation (D) Escrow balance held by the seller's lender	A
33	If the sale of a foreclosed home fails to fulfill the mortgage, the lender may file a lawsuit against the buyer and... (A) may file a deed in lieu of foreclosure. (B) may go to court and seek a deficiency judgment. (C) has no way to recover additional money from the person in default. (D) may allow the person in default of the mortgage to exercise the right of reversion	B
34	For the buyer, which of the following items is NOT covered by the seller's home warranty insurance? (A) Heating system (B) Dishwasher (C) Roof repairs (D) Foundation	D
35	During the year 2009, William Jones sold his home for $587,000. He had purchased the home in 1975 for a sum of $743,257. What is the rate of depreciation or appreciation on a yearly basis? (A) 26.6% appreciates B) 26.6% depreciates (C) 0.8% appreciates (D) 0.8% depreciates	D
36	A real estate agent should examine the following factors while doing a competitive market analysis: (A) only the prices of homes in your area that sold within the last 60 days.	D

	(B) only the prices of homes in your area that sold within the last 6 months. (C) the prices of homes that sold and did not sell in your area within the 6 months. (D) the prices of homes that sold and did not sell in your area within the shortest time practical based on the number of listings and sales.	
37	After purchasing a property from the Jacksons, the Stephens were not informed that the woods behind the home would be demolished to make room for a 500-unit townhouse development. The Stephens's are a family of writers, they... (A) can sue to void the contract because of nondisclosure on the part of the Jacksons. (B) can claim the contract is voidable because of fraud and sue to rescind it. (C) can claim that the contract is invalid because they have lost the right of quiet enjoyment of their property. (D) have only two options: to stay in the house or try to sell it.	B
38	When does a purchase and sale agreement between a buyer and a seller become legally binding? (A) The buyer's agent gives the seller's agent the buyer's offer. (B) The seller accepts the buyer's offer. (C) The buyer's agent tells the buyer of the seller's acceptance. (D) The buyer's agent tells the seller's agent that the buyer has been notified.	C
39	The following are some of the responsibilities that a realtor is responsible for: EXCEPT (A) providing information about local property taxes. (B) making sure that the inspections have been carried out. (C) having the title and mortgage recorded after the closing. (D) providing an estimate of closing costs.	C
40	Sam Schieffer is interested in renting an apartment for his mother, who is in her eighties and a widow. He is requesting that the landlord grant him permission to put grab bars near the toilet and in the bathtub. Under the terms of what lease, the landlord must consent? (A) Fair Housing Act. (B) Americans with Disabilities Act. (C) Rehabilitation Act of 1973. (D) Housing and Community Development Act of 1981	A
41	Adam's home will be purchased by Susan and Jay Morton, who have signed the sales agreement. A statement is made to the Morton's indicating that they now hold equitable title to the land, which transfers (A) complete ownership to the buyer. (B) property free and clear of encumbrances. (C) joint ownership to a married couple.	D

	(D) the right to complete ownership.	
42	An appraiser's report contains all of the information below WITH THE EXCEPTION OF (A) type of value estimated. (B) data gathered and analyzed in appraising the property. (C) insurance information. (D) the purpose for the appraisal.	C
43	Dina Stewart decided she wanted to go from the suburbs to the city and listed her home for sale. She received an offer from Phelps and accepted it, signing the sales contract in the process. After that, she had a change of heart. While everything was going on, the Phelps found that they were expecting another child and felt that Dina's home was too small for them. Both parties spoke about their sentiments and came to an agreement on how to proceed. What did they do? (A) remainder the contract (B) liquidate the contract (C) rescind the contract. (D) accept compensatory damages.	C
44	According to federal regulations governing underground storage tanks, which of the following is NOT covered? (A) Gas station oil tanks (B) Home heating oil tanks (C) Chemical plant tanks (D) Used motor oil tanks	B
45	Jack Patton has gone into an option to purchase a deal with the Benjamin Corporation in order to purchase a 320-acre block of property on which to develop condominiums. According to this circumstance, which of the following claims is correct? (A) Patton has an obligation to buy the land. (B) The Benjamin is under no obligation to sell the land to Patton. (C) The Benjamin has an obligation to sell the land to Patton. (D) With an option to buy, the price is not set, so Patton and the Benjamin still have to negotiate a price acceptable to both parties.	C
46	Joe Spires wants to sell his land so that it may be developed. If the farm has a total land area of 5,445,000 square feet, how many 1.5-acre lots may he offer to the developer as a proposal? (A) 186 (B) 189 (C) 188 (D) 187	D
47	In a state whose mortgage law is based on the notion of ownership... (A) the mortgagor turns over legal title to the mortgagee.	A

| | (B) the mortgagor retains the legal title, and the mortgagee retains the deed.
 (C) a lien is placed on the property.
 (D) the mortgagee receives equitable title. | |

Practice Test 3

Question Number	Question	Answer
1	The Hammers, an African American couple interested in purchasing their first home, are being shown around by a realtor in mostly African American neighborhoods. This is referred to as an example of (A) blockbusting. (B) steering. (C) redlining. (D) curtailment.	B
2	It is possible to remove a cloud from a title in certain circumstances. (A) a quitclaim deed. (B) title insurance. (C) a special warranty. (D) judicial warranty.	A
3	A/an executory contract is a/an agreement between two or more parties to be carried out. (A) sales contract used by an executor in selling an estate. (B) contract in which the obligation is in the future. (C) contract used in an eminent domain proceeding. (D) employment contract between a property management company and a real estate holding company.	B
4	The Reynolds' house is assessed at $340,000, which is 85 percent of its market value, according to the appraisal. Their annual property taxes amount to around $4,760. Was this a positive or negative impact on their monthly mortgage payment? (A) $3.96 (B) $39.96 (C) $396.67 (D) There is not enough information to answer the question	C

5	Frank's Hardware Store has signed a gross lease agreement with the property owner. Frank has agreed to reimburse the costs. (A) rent based on the business's receipts. (B) rent, utilities, and real estate taxes only. (C) rent and possibly utilities. (D) rent, real estate taxes, and repair and maintenance to the premises.	C
6	An ARM may have all of the following characteristics WITHOUT THE FEATURES LISTED BELOW. (A) interest rate adjustment cap. (B) life of loan interest rate adjustment cap. (C) periodic interest rate change. (D) recalculation of the principal periodically.	D
7	The saleswoman and the broker divided the commission on the sale of Jon Restivo's property, according to Sion. In the case of a home that sold for $239,000 with a 5.75 percent commission and a broker who received 60 percent of the commission, what is the saleswoman's percentage of commission? (A) $549.70 (B) $5,497 (C) $8,245.50 (D) $13,742.50	B
8	The loss of real estate as a consequence of a buyer's violation of a sales contract is referred to as a breach of contract. (A) foreclosure. (B) forfeiture. (C) default. (D) renunciation.	B
9	The method that makes use of an abstract of title comes to a close with (A) the issuance of a deed. (B) a certificate of title being issued. (C) an attorney's opinion of the title. (D) issuance of a certificate of Torrens.	C
10	Which of the following deed restrictions would be unenforceable in a mixed-use planned unit development? (A) Building height (B) Type of business (C) Religious affiliation (D) Lot size	C
11	Mark Jonas is an experienced realtor who continuously qualifies prospective buyers by asking them a series of qualifying questions about (A) about their educational background and jobs. (B) about their financial situation. (C) why they want to buy.	B

	(D) where they want to buy and for how much.	
12	Property owners who hold shares in the underlying corporation are entitled to get which of the following? (A) Townhome (B) Condo (C) PUD (D) Co-op	D
13	Is it possible to calculate the yearly interest rate on a loan for $92,000 based on the interest paid for the first three months of the loan, which was $2,300? (A) 12% (B) 1% (C) 10% (D) 8%	C
14	Which of the following is the most accurate definition of a leasehold estate? (A) Estate for years (B) Life estate purpure vie (C) Qualified fee determinable (D) Defeasible estate	A
15	The phrase "riparian rights" refers to the rights that rivers and streams have over their surroundings... (A) those who own property along rivers and streams. (B) those who own beachfront and lake- front property. (C) commercial fishermen to fish within the 12-mile offshore limit. (D) shore communities to zone beach- front property.	A
16	All of the elements listed below are often addressed in zoning laws and regulations. EXCEPT (A) number of rooms. (B) setback. (C) number of floors. (D) square footage.	A
17	It is possible that the contract of sale will contain a provision saying that, if an inspection finds a pest infestation, the seller must remedy the situation and provide evidence to the buyer, or the buyer may choose to stop the transaction and get their deposit back. This is referred to as a/an.... in formal language. (A) inclusion. (B) contingency. (C) condition of sale. (D) restriction.	B
18	On a property with an appraised value of $132,000, an 80 percent loan of the property's worth was made available. The annual percentage rate of interest is 4.38 percent. What is the amount of interest that will be paid in 6 months? (A) $2,312.64	A

	(B) $23,126.40 (C) $4,625.28 (D) $2,890.80	
19	According to this question, which of the following is a social component that influences the value of a home? (A) Corner influence (B) Local economy (C) Proximity to the subway (D) Type of restaurants and shops	D
20	True or incorrect about a typical life estate is which of the following statements about it? (A) Death can terminate an ordinary life estate. (B) An ordinary life estate can be leased to another party. (C) An ordinary life estate can be sold, but not mortgaged. (D) An ordinary life estate cannot be willed to another person.	C
21	All of the items listed below must be included in the Good Faith Estimate, with the exception of (A) loan discount points. (B) property taxes—city and county. (C) appraisal fee. (D) realtor's commission.	D
22	It is not necessary to get PMI if the buyer is ready to pay for it. (A) puts down 10 percent of the purchase price and has a fixed rate mortgage. (B) finances no more than 80 percent of the purchase price. (C) is making monthly payments that are less than 28 percent of the buyer's income. (D) has a credit score of at least 700.	B
23	For tax purposes, how much is the taxable value of a property on Main Street that is appraised at $1,342,900 and assessed at 73 percent of its market value? (A) $98,031.70 (B) $980,317 (C) $9,803 170 (D) $9,803.17	B
24	A straight-term mortgage is a loan in which the borrower repays the amount over a predetermined length of time, such as 30 years. (A) the loan off in regular installments over the term of the mortgage. (B) interest only on the mortgage over the term of the mortgage. (C) the mortgage off early without incurring a prepayment penalty. (D) a fixed monthly payment for a period of years and then adjusted rates for a period of years	B

25	Noah and his family have lived in their home for 20 years. The value of the property has increased from $152,000 to $312,000. Generally speaking, the difference is defined as the amount of difference between the purchase price and the current price, minus any residual mortgage balance. (A) equitable title. (B) dividend. (C) equity. (D) investment value	C
26	According to the Fair Housing Act, which of the following individuals is not considered to be a protected class in the housing market? (A) A person with an IQ of 65 (B) A person with cerebral palsy (C) An active heroin addicts (D) An active alcoholic	C
27	In accordance with state legislation, some states require that real estate sales contracts must be in writing before closing. (A) Statute of Frauds. (B) Statute of Delivery. (C) Real Estate Commission regulations. (D) Statute of Liability.	A
28	In accordance with the Truth in Lending Act, every one of the following must be disclosed to a borrower. EXCEPT (A) annual percentage rate. (B) amount of finance charges. (C) prepayment penalties. (D) credit score.	D
29	Identify which of the following assertions about Veterans Administration-backed mortgages is accurate. (A) The mortgagor must be on active duty. (B) The mortgagor will not have to pay monthly mortgage insurance. (C) The mortgagor must put down at least 10 percent. (D) The mortgagor will have to pay a prepayment penalty if the mortgage is paid off early. 80	B
30	On August 10th, for $133,000, a $751 payment for a three-year insurance policy was made. On June 1 of the previous year, a payment for a three-year insurance policy was made for $751. Is there any money owed to the seller by the buyer? (A) $451.87 (B) $0.00 (C) $299.13 (D) $345.91	A
31	Oliver's property is 82 feet in width. Side yard setbacks must be a minimum of 10 feet on each side and a total of at least 25 feet	C

	for both side yards to be considered acceptable. What is the greatest width that the Oliver's proposed home may be before they must apply for a variance from the township? (A) 57 feet (B) 62 feet (C) 67 feet (D) 72 feet	
32	Specifically, what kind of variance would the Oliver's be required to submit for if their side yard setbacks are too narrow? (A) Use (B) Special permit (C) Conforming (D) Area	D
33	In the case of Bernadette James, who just sold her home for $748,231, and who purchased it for $347,295 fifteen years ago, what is the yearly rate of appreciation? (A) $400,936 (B) $40,936 (C) 8% (D) 1.15	C
34	They jointly acquire a large number of townhouses for use as rental units, with tenancy in common serving as the ownership structure in most cases. Following the Lloyds' divorce, Sara Lloyd sells her ownership stake in the townhouses to a third party. Is she capable of doing this task successfully? (A) Yes, because tenancy in common allows a co-owner to sell his or her interest. (B) Yes, if she made it a provision of her divorce settlement. (C) Yes, but only if she lived in a com- munity property state. (D) Yes, if she obtained the agreement of her ex-husband and Luca.	A
35	When a person is evicted in a constructive manner, it is referred to as constructive eviction. (A) a landlord removes a tenant who refuses to leave the premises at the expiration of the lease. (B) a landlord neglects the premises so badly that it becomes uninhabitable. (C) a landlord expels a tenant who has complained to the authorities about the landlord's neglect of the premises. (D) a building has been damaged through no fault of the tenant or landlord and the tenant has to move because of renovation or rebuilding.	B
36	When it comes to building data, what kind of information do appraisers like to see the most? (A) Costs (B) Taxes (C) Market value	A

	(D) Real estate closings	
37	Gerald and Shirley Basile have agreed to donate their house to the Bronx Zoo on the condition that it be utilized as a conservation center for the animals there. Do you know what kind of involvement the Bronx Zoo has with the Basils' property? (A) Estate at will (B) Testate (C) Estate at sufferance (D) Determinable	D
38	Earlier this month, a colonial-style property in New market sold for $465,380. It has a total floor area of 2,740 square feet and has 5 bedrooms and 3.5 bathrooms. In New market, there is a colonial with 5 bedrooms, 3.5 bathrooms, and 2,846 square feet that is on the market. What is the monetary value of it? (A) $465,380 (B) $483,393 (C) $465,549 (D) $479,424	B
39	If the sale of a similar property took place more than one year ago, an appraiser would not consider it to be a credible market signal for the purposes of valuing the subject property. (A) month ago. (B) sixty days ago. (C) ninety days ago. (D) six months ago.	D
40	There is no difference between the insurable value and market value of a property. (A) assessed value. (B) appraised value. (C) reimbursement value. (D) market value.	C
41	A jumbo loan is a loan that is much bigger than a typical loan in size. (A) another name for an 80/20 mortgage. (B) a mortgage that is larger than the limit to qualify for a government- insured low-interest loan (C) a package of loans sold on the secondary mortgage market. (D) another name for a wraparound mortgage.	B
42	Using an acreage that sells for $17,500 per acre and an assessed value of 63 percent, what is the tax rate on a 90' by 363' property that sells for $17,500 per acre? (A) $394.82 (B) $463.89 (C) $564.37 (D) $355.56	D

| 43 | Which of the following circumstances would not be covered by the Fair Housing Act's protections against discrimination?
(A) A landlord renting an apartment in a four-unit building
(B) A FSBO property
(C) A developer selling townhouses in a PUD (D) Nuns who run an assisted living facility for the elderly and accept public funding | B |

| 44 | It will be necessary for the Forman father-and-son garment firm to sell their storefront property in order to pay off its obligations. This is referred to as a slang term.
(A) forfeiture sale.
(B) liquidation sale.
(C) tax sale.
(D) foreclosure. | B |

45	What is the Truth-in-Lending Act, and why should homebuyers be concerned about it? (A) It details how the Good Faith Estimate is to be calculated. (B) It specifies how the amortization rate on a mortgage should be calculated. (C) It spells out how the annual per- centage rate of a loan should be calculated and stated in loan documents. (D) It established an agency to supervise mortgage lenders.	C
46	A deed that does not include a warranty is known as a non-guaranteed deed. (A) unencumbered deed. (B) quitclaim deed. (C) sheriff's deed. (D) referee's deed in foreclosure.	B
47	A worn-out, unclean carpet would be taken into consideration during an examination as (A) an incurable functional obsolescence. (B) a curable physical deterioration. (C) an incurable economic obsolescence. (D) a curable functional obsolescence.	B
48	Which of the following would NOT be included in a legal property description created using the rectangle survey technique? (A) Principal meridian (B) Location of physical features (C) Baseline (D) Direction	B
49	When a property is condemned, the procedure of transferring title to a real estate developer is carried out on the site. (A) adverse possession (B) involuntary alienation. (C) escheat.	B

	(D) assignment.	

Practice Test 4

Question Number	Question	Answer
1	Tony Willow owns a triangular plot of property that is just across the street from the park. His land was worth $324,000 dollars to him. If a piece of land has a frontage of 173 feet and a depth of 86 feet, how much did he pay per square foot and how many acres does he own? A) $45.97 per square foot; 1/3 of an acre (B) $7.44 per square foot; 1/3 of an acre (C) $7.44 per square foot; 1/6 of an acre (D) $45.97 per square foot; 1/6 of an acre	D
2	All of the following are actions that are prohibited under the Truth-in-Lending Act, with the exception of : (A) RESPA. (B) Good Faith Estimate. (C) Regulation Z. (D) Statute of Frauds.	D
3	William James has been living in a hut in the woods on the Benjamin's property with their permission for the last 15 years, but he hasn't paid rent in that time. When both Benjamin pass away, their heirs want to expel Kiley from the house. He asserts that the property is his as a result of (A) assumption. (B) assignment. (C) escheat. (D) adverse possession.	D
4	The Premier Painting Company is the company that Sam Lawrence recommends to his clients when a home has to be painted before it is placed on the market. Lawrence receives a fee from the painting company for each assignment that he introduces to them. This is referred to as a slang term. (A) transfer fee. (B) kickback. (C) logrolling.	B

	(D) bandwagon.	
5	When may a utility provider place an encumbrance on a piece of real estate? (A) Easement by prescription (B) Easement in gross (C) Mechanic's lien (D) Easement by necessity	B
6	A contract established with a mentally ill individual is nonetheless considered to be a legal contract. (A) voidable contract. (B) valid, but unenforceable contract. (C) void contract. (D) voidable, but enforceable contract.	C
7	When purchasing a $435,000 house, a fee of $19,575 is levied. What is the percentage of commission earned? (A) 0.035 (B) 0.045 (C) 0.055 (D) 0.065	B
8	A charge of $19,575 is levied on a $435,000 home, for a total cost of $435,000. When it comes to commissions, how much does it cost? (A) $673.75 (B) $67,375 (C) $6,737.50 (D) $673,750	B
9	If you use metes and bounds to describe a legal property, which of the following is NOT included in the description? (A) Distance (B) Baseline (C) Point of beginning (D) Direction	B
10	Sharon Macy and Ben Porter are purchasing a home jointly before tying the knot, and they have spoken with their agent about the kind of ownership they should commit to. They should be notified by the real estate agent. (A) to check their state's real estate laws to see if they can use tenancy in entirety. (B) that the best option is to be listed as domestic partners. (C) to check with an attorney. (D) that the best option is to be listed as a partnership.	C
11	Purchasing a home together before getting married, Sharon Macy and Ben Porter question their real estate agent the sort of ownership	D

	they should choose for. This responsibility falls on the shoulders of the realtor. (A) MLS (B) Net listing (C) Dual agency (D) Open listing	
12	The buyer has the choice to make a buying decision. (A) the right to purchase a particular property. (B) the obligation to purchase a particular property. (C) the right and the obligation to purchase a particular property. (D) a specified time during which the buyer and seller can work out terms to purchase a particular property.	A
13	The income approach of valuing a property is based on the concept of future earnings. (A) conformity. (B) contribution. (C) anticipation. (D) substitution.	C
14	Who is responsible for paying the discount points on the mortgage loan at the time of closing? (A) Buyer (B) Seller (C) Buyer or seller, depending on how the sale contract is negotiated (D) No points are paid at closing; they wrap into the mortgage	C
15	The word "debt liquidation" refers to the process of paying off a debt that has been incurred. (A) amortization. (B) depreciation. (C) rescission. (D) seisin.	A
16	"Debt liquidation" is the term used to describe the process of paying off a debt. (A) 20 percent loan in an 80/20 mortgage (B) Largest mortgage amount (C) First mortgage to be recorded (D) Back taxes	C
17	Identify which of the following statements about tenancy in common is accurate. (A) Tenancy in common requires that ownership be split 50/50. (B) Tenancy in common is the most frequent form of joint ownership. (C) A person who owns property in tenancy in common may not mortgage his or her interest without the consent of the other party or parties. (D) Tenancy in common confers the right of survivorship.	B

18	The term "functional obsolescence" refers to the state of being no longer useful. (A) one bathroom in a three-bedroom house. (B) a crack in the basement floor. (C) the lack of a built-in barbecue in the backyard. (D) white wall paint in all the rooms.	A
19	When evaluating a property, the URAR is used. (A) single-family residence. (B) condominium. (C) co-op unit. (D) commercial property other than residential rentals.	A
20	In a legal description of real estate, which of the following elements is not included: (A) Monument description of the property (B) Street address of the property (C) Lot and block system (D) Metes and bounds system	B
21	The usual relationship between a listing agent and a seller is a/an. (A) universal agency. (B) agency with interest. (C) special agency. (D) general agency.	C
22	When the township tax rate is 22 mills and the school district tax rate is 29 mills, what are the taxes on a $75,000 property that is assessed at 67 percent of its value? (A) $351.75 (B) $1,105.50 (C) $1,457.25 (D) $2,562.75	D
23	A property manager is a person who is in charge of the management of real estate. (A) must be a certified property manager. (B) must be a licensed real estate agent or broker. (C) does not need to be licensed . (D) must at the least be working toward a license	B
24	When determining if something is a fixture, one of the requirements is to ask which of the following questions? (A) How is the item attached? (B) Who attached the item? (C) Can the item be removed? (D) How long has the item been attached?	A
25	What is the purpose of recording deeds after closings? (A) As the final step in filing title insurance (B) As part of the mortgage process (C) To give public notice that the title has passed	C

	(D) As the final step in passing title from seller to buyer	
26	Sarah Mayfield, the proprietor of the Sally Mae Shop, enters into an agreement with Shepherd Realty to lease a storefront. Sarah is solely responsible for the payment of her utilities and real estate taxes. She has almost certainly signed a contract. (A) percentage lease. (B) net lease. (C) double net lease. (D) gross lease.	B
27	The Oliver's have chosen to put their flat on the market. They've been bargaining with Brad Morse and bouncing back and forth between the two of them. Brad has decided to walk away from the situation after rejecting the most recent counteroffer. The Thomas's are a family of four and (A) can attempt to restart the negotiations by making a new, lower offer. (B) can accept the last counteroffer from Brad prior to their counteroffer. (C) can take their counteroffer off the table. (D) have no action they can take.	A
28	The sale of the community barbershop took place on March 12. What much is owed by the seller to the buyer if the quarterly taxes of $456.84 have not been paid by the seller? (A) $153.28 (B) $304.56 (C) $360.40 (D) $456.84	C
29	Which of the following characteristics is included in a legal deed? (A) Habendum clause (B) Mutual agreement (C) Warranty (D) Legal purpose	A
30	Except for the following, any of the following may result in the termination of a listing agreement: (A) revocation. (B) bankruptcy. (C) remainder men. (D) eminent domain.	C
31	Phase II of the environmental investigation comprises the following activities: (A) history of the property. (B) actual cleanup of primary contaminants. (C) sampling and analysis of the site. (D) site management plan.	C

32	The federal government proposes to construct a dam on the Sawtooth River in Idaho. What documentation does the Army Corps of Engineers need to provide before they can proceed? (A) List of endangered species on the site (B) Two alternative building plans (C) Environmental impact statement (D) Environmental rehabilitation plan	C

33	~~This is an example of~~ which of the following is a kind of family status discrimination? (A) Refusal to rent to a husband and wife over 60 (B) Refusal to rent to a Korean husband and wife (C) Refusal to rent to an African American husband and wife and the man's mother (D) Refusal to rent to a gay couple with two-year-old twins	D
34	In order to buy their house, Lucas secured a mortgage from First National Bank of New York. During the closing, Luca signs the mortgage and the deed of trust on his behalf. (A) note. (B) title. (C) deed. (D) commission checks to the broker.	A
35	The straight-line approach of calculating depreciation is the most accurate way to utilize... (A) physical deterioration. (B) functional obsolescence. (C) economic obsolescence. (D) external obsolescence.	A
36	Several pieces of land from a variety of landowners have been acquired by William in order to construct a big enough lot for their home, which is 10,000 square feet in size. Combining lots is the term used to describe the practice of merging lots. (A) best use. (B) pottage. (C) plat. (D) special use.	B
37	When it comes to a listing agreement, which of the following is not mandatory? (A) Price (B) Signature of the broker (C) Commission (D) Form of termination	D
38	This term refers to the use of a property before the introduction of zoning regulations, which would have made the use unlawful. This is referred to as a "pre-zoning use." (A) conditional use.	B

	(B) nonconforming use. (C) non conventional use. (D) accessory use.	
39	Gus Luca purchased his home in 1989 for $84,927 and sold it in 2009 for $113,908 – a difference of $84,927. The amount by which the residence appreciated or depreciated is important. (A) Depreciate by $198,835 (B) Depreciate by $28,981 (C) Appreciate by $28,981 (D) Appreciate by $198,835	C
40	The trait that distinguishes fraud from other forms of deception is... (A) unknowing ignorance of the facts. (B) failure to learn about the property being shown. (C) intent to deceive. (D) imparting mistaken information.	C
41	It is the overall interest rate of a loan, including all charges and fees, that is known as the effective rate. (A) APR. (B) APY. (C) API. (D) APAR	A
42	Which of the following statements about dual agency is untrue and why? (A) Conflict of interest is inherent in a dual agency arrangement. (B) In a dual agency, one broker or agent represents both parties in a real estate sale. (C) Dual agency is legal in all 50 states. (D) Dual agency must be disclosed to both parties in a real estate sale.	C
43	What are some instances of the agent's obligations to the principal, such as obedience, loyalty, confidentiality, and correct accounting? (A) Fiduciary (B) Agency (C) Transactional (D) Bundle	A
44	Julie William is interested in a Cape Cod-style house that is identical to a Cape Cod that sold up the street last month in every way except that the comparable property has a completely finished basement, but the property she is interested in has a 25 percent finished basement. What is the value of the home Julie is contemplating purchasing if the house has a completely finished basement worth $17,900 and the comparable property sold for $231,00? (A) $217,575 (B) $213,100 (C) $247,575	A

	(D) $244,425 practice	
45	In an exclusive agency listing with Morgan Realty, Marty Chu has joined on with the firm. Martin sells his home on his own, without the assistance of Morgan Realty. Is Marty required to pay a commission to Morgan Realty? (A) Yes, because he listed the property with Morgan Realty. (B) Yes, but it's only 50 percent of the agreed-upon commission. (C) No, because under an exclusive agreement, the realtor only gets a commission if the realtor sells the property. (D) Only if Marty sold the property for more than he listed it with Morgan.	C
46	The following are the components of the cost approach of property evaluation: (A) the value of the land plus the cost to build the improvements (new), less depreciation of the improvements. (B) the value of the land plus the cost to build the improvements (new), less appreciation of the improvements. (C) the value of the land, less deep- citation of the improvements. (D) the value of the land plus the cost to build the improvements (originally), less depreciation.	A
47	An appraiser is evaluating a townhouse that has a new tile kitchen floor as well as all new stainless-steel kitchen appliances and equipment. Two bedrooms, a loft, and a fireplace can be found in this house. He located a similar property with the same layout, but the kitchen floor is linoleum that is 20 years old, and the appliances are also 20 years old. He decided to purchase the home. The following information will be required by the appraiser. (A) discard this comp and find one with the same value as the subject property. (B) adjust the value of the comp upward (C) adjust the value of the subject house downward. (D) adjust the value of the subject house downward and the value of the comp upward to fall within a certain range.	B
48	Olive's Organic Food Store is moving to a new location. Olive desires to move her shelves and counters to a more convenient location. Her landlord has told her that she would be unable to fulfil her obligations. Who is proper in this situation? (A) Olive, because she paid for the improvements (B) The landlord, because these are now attached to the property and are, therefore, fixtures (C) Olive, because she signed a com- metrical lease and under the lease, the fixtures can be removed and the premises returned to the original condition (D) The landlord, because removing them will increase the wear and tear on the property	C

Practice Test 5

Question Number	Question	Answer
1	The buyer is required to pass over the necessary documents at the time of the sales contract signing. (A) the down payment. (B) earnest money. (C) part of the down payment. (D) a note for the down payment.	B
2	All of the following restrictive covenants in a townhouse development are likely to increase the value of the homes in the community. EXCEPT (A) the color of the exterior front door and window trim. (B) how long outdoor Christmas lights may be used. (C) the type of planters that may be used outdoors. (D) the distance that woodpiles may be kept from the dwellings.	B
3	The loan amount, granting clause, and season covenant are all frequently contained in the loan agreement. (A) mortgage note. (B) mortgage document itself. (C) title to the property. (D) deed to the property.	B
4	A typical listing agreement comprises all of the provisions listed below WITH THE EXCEPTION OF (A) type of zoning. (B) assessment and taxes. (C) nondiscrimination clause. (D) description of how the realtor arrived at the sales price.	D
5	When a material flaw occurs in a property, an example might be (A) a 100-year-old electrical system. (B) the addition of an attic fan that was not done to building code. (C) cracked and peeling paint from water damage from an upstairs bathtub that overflowed. (D) the presence of squirrel droppings in the attic.	A
6	What kind of depreciation is shown by the response to Question 5? (A) Physical deterioration (B) Functional obsolescence (C) Economic obsolescence (D) Effective age	B
7	Sara Jeffs has an agreement with a local real estate company under which she receives 65 percent of the 45 percent in commissions she	C

	produces on sales. What was the amount of Sara's commission check at the end of the month if she sold two properties in May for a total of $790,000, with each property receiving a 6 percent commission split between the broker and the salesperson? (A) $1,386.45 (B) $2,133.00 (C) $13,864.50 (D) $47,400.00	
8	A designated agency is one that has been designated... (A) one in which the buyer signs a buyer agency agreement and the seller signs a listing agreement with the same broker. (B) one in which a broker has exclusive rights to sell all the units for a developer (C) the same as a dual agency. (D) the same as an exclusive right to sell listing given by any principal to a broker.	A
9	The MPI is an acronym that stands for the Ministry of Public Instruction. (A) a form of private mortgage insurance. (B) a one-time insurance premium on FHA-insured mortgages. (C) equal to one point on a mortgage. (D) an abbreviation for mortgage, principal, and interest.	B
10	In order to close, the borrower must give over to the lender a certain number of months' worth of all of the following payments, which the lender must deposit into an escrow account. EXCEPT (A) county property taxes. (B) municipal property taxes. (C) interest. (D) hazard insurance premiums.	C
11	An estate with an undetermined lifespan is referred to as a/an (A) estate from period to period. (B) freehold estate. (C) leasehold estate. (D) estate at will.	B
12	Joe Rex just celebrated his 75th birthday. This qualifies him to a 20 percent tax credit on his local property taxes in his township. What would his new tax bill be if his home and property are valued at $675,000, and the township assesses at a rate of 84 percent and taxes are assessed at a cost of $4.50 per thousand dollars? (A) $2,143.90 (B) $2,987.20 (C) $2,551.50 (D) $2,041.20	D
13	An advertisement that contains one of the following terms is considered to be full disclosure in the loan advertising industry. (A) Terms of repayment (B) Annual percentage rate	D

	(C) Availability of FHA and VA loans (D) Dollar amount of finance charge	
14	The company Schultz Realty employs Cherry Oilex as a real estate agent. One of the homes he is attempting to sell is being advertised in the local newspaper. A legal requirement for the advertisement is that it include which of the following items: (A) Address of the property (B) Sales price (C) Property taxes (D) Name of the broker for whom he works	D
15	A copy of which of the following documents must be sent to mortgage applicants one day before the closing date? (A) Uniform Residential Appraisal Report (B) Good Faith Estimate (C) Uniform Residential Loan Application (D) HUD-1, or Uniform Settlement Statement	D
16	Lenders may take legal action against homeowners who fail to sell their repossessed homes in order to fulfil their mortgage obligations... (A) may file a deed in lieu of foreclosure. (B) may go to court and seek a deficiency judgment. (C) has no way to recover additional money from the person in default. (D) may allow the person in default of the mortgage to exercise the right of reversion.	B
17	The condo costs of $215.46 per month are payable on the first of every month, unless otherwise specified. Erin Oskin sells her apartment to Jake Otis on October 16; how much does Jake owe Erin as a result of the sale? (A) $3,447.36 (B) $114.88 (C) $123.62 (D) $107.73	D
18	In order to assess a property, Marry William is using the cost technique. This method includes the cost of construction, depreciation, and amortization. (A) appreciation. (B) value of the land. (C) value of the improvement. (D) income.	B
19	A representative comes to the Baileys' farm to see whether they are interested in selling it. When the Baileys agree, they ask the agency to locate a buyer on their behalf. There is no listing agreement in place. This oral agreement is a formal agreement. (A) is not enforceable. (B) may be enforceable if their state's Statute of Frauds recognizes oral contracts. (C) is enforceable if the broker agrees to accept an oral contract.	B

	(D) may be enforceable if their state's Real Estate Commission recognizes oral contracts.	
20	A lender maintains the right to refuse a loan application. (A) hire an appraiser during the term of a mortgage to ensure that the mortgagor is maintaining the property. (B) approve any substantive changes to a property by the mortgagor during the term of the mortgage. (C) approve the sale of the property. (D) approve a lessee for the property during the term of the mortgage.	B
21	What was the selling price of a home if it sold for 165 percent of its initial value of $431,970, or $431,970? (A) $261,800 (B) $316,782 (C) $587,920 (D) $712,750	D
22	Who is responsible for writing the cheques for prorated monies awarded to the seller after a closing? (A) Buyer (B) Buyer's broker (C) Buyer's attorney (D) Whoever is acting as escrow agent	D
23	Sellers should examine all of the following factors in addition to price when assessing numerous bids, with the exception of the price. (A) closing dates. (B) amounts of the down payments. (C) contingencies. (D) whether the buyer is relocating.	D
24	Lot size, building height, and other aspects of development are all governed by zoning rules. (A) layout of municipal transportation systems. (B) distance between structures on adjoining properties. (C) weight limits on residential streets. (D) building codes.	B
25	One advantage of a VA-guaranteed loan is that it is more affordable. (A) the VA guarantees that the home is free of defects. (B) the VA can order builders to fix problems with construction problems. (C) private mortgage insurance is waived. (D) down payments as low as 3 percent qualify for a mortgage.	C
26	An escrow account for the purpose of obtaining a mortgage (A) is regulated under the Truth-in- Lending Act. (B) may not keep in the account more than one-sixth of the total amount necessary to be paid out, or approximately two months of escrow funds. (C) is mandated by RESPA.	B

	(D) must pay interest to the borrower on the money in the account.	
27	Which of the following does not constitute a responsibility of a real estate broker? (A) Hire home inspectors (B) Arrange for title searches (C) Help the buyer to obtain financing (D) Act as closing agent	A
28	A triplex went for $329,000, according to the listing. What is the rate of return on an investment property that earns $37,500 in revenue each year? (A) 9.6% (B) 10.3% (C) 11.4% (D) 877%	C
29	The Ace Chemical Company has been informed that the pollution in its old facility would not be able to be cleaned up by conventional means. What degree of environmental research does the corporation need to contract out at this point? (A) Phase I (B) Phase II (C) Phase III (D) Phase IV	D
30	The Homeowner's Protection Act defines a residential mortgage transaction as one in which the borrower lives in the home. (A) is a single-family dwelling. (B) has from 1 to 4 units. (C) has a VA-guaranteed or FHA-insured mortgage. (D) has a fixed rate mortgage.	A
31	The Oliver's have purchased a tract of unimproved property in a single-family residential neighborhood with the intention of constructing a two-family structure. They will be located on one side of the building, while Mona Hudson's parents will be located on the opposite side of the structure. The Oliver's have a pressing need to find a/an (A) nonconforming use variance. (B) area variance. (C) use variance. (D) accessory building variance	C
32	Under RESPA, a homebuyer enjoys all of the following rights, with the exception of the ability to negotiate a lower price. (A) compare the cost of mortgages from different lenders. (B) refuse to allow the mortgagee to sell the mortgage to a mortgage servicer. (C) know which charges are refundable if the buyer cancels the loan agreement. (D) know how much a mortgage broker is being paid by the lender.	B

33	Property on a square plot was originally sold for $2.55 per square foot when the land was first purchased. Currently, the price per square foot is $3.75 per square foot. Can you tell me how much the property has valued, given that it has a frontage of 752 feet? (A) $664,706.90 (B) $678,604.80 (C) $682,763.90 (D) $693,874.80	B
34	What percentage of the property's worth was set aside by the DHA as the maximum amount of help a seller may provide to a buyer? (A) 2.25 percent (B) 3 percent (C) 6 percent (D) 10 percent	B
35	A mortgage note normally includes all of the information listed below, WITH THE EXCEPTION of the following: (A) interest rate of the mortgage. (B) date on which the note was signed. (C) names of the seller and buyer . (D) day of the month on which mortgage payments are due.	C
36	A mortgage that is energy efficient... (A) can be used to fund a condo. (B) cannot fund improvements that increase the mortgage by more than $2,500. (C) cannot fund improvements that will add more than 10 percent to the value of the property. (D) enables a homebuyer to save money on future utility bills.	D
37	When it comes to paying off liens, the right sequence is as follows: (A) IRS, liens by contractors, property tax liens. (B) property tax liens, IRS, liens by contractors. (C) IRS, state tax liens, property tax liens. (D) property tax liens, IRS, state tax liens.	C
38	The total amount of interest paid on a $265,000, 15-year loan with a monthly payment of $2,011.02 is equal to the following: (A) $96,983.60 (B) $9,698.36 (C) $969,836.00 (D) $9,698,360.00	A
39	The neighborhood gas station was sold for $953,252 on January 26th. In the case of real estate taxes of $5,348.24 that are paid quarterly on the first of January, April, July, and October, how much does the buyer owe the original homeowners? (A) $965.68 (B) $1,139.74 (C) $1,262.88 (D) $4,976.89	A

40	Which of the following phrases would be deemed a violation of the Fair Housing Act if they were used in a rental unit advertisement? (A) "Master bedroom end suite" (B) "Older woman preferred" (C) "Walk to subway" (D) "Bachelor apartment"	B
41	Seepage is a potential danger associated with a/an leach field. (A) septic system. (B) fuel tank to supply oil to the furnace. (C) cesspool. (D) in-ground swimming pool.	A
42	A house inspection does not often include an examination of which of the following factors: (A) Structural (B) Mechanical (C) Energy efficiency (D) Environmental	C
43	All of the items listed below are commonly contained in a home inspection contingency provision in a sales contract, with the exception of the last item. (A) buyer satisfaction with the repairs. (B) statement of how any repairs will be made. (C) how many days the seller has to make the repairs after the home inspection report is received. (D) the buyer's choice to go ahead with the purchase even if the repairs are not made.	B
44	It cost $87,000 to construct a home on $17,000 lot three years ago, according to the latest available figures. Currently, what is the entire property worth, assuming that a house depreciates at 1.7% per year and a piece of land increases at 6.5 percent per year? (A) $99,563 (B) $102,878 (C) $112,615 (D) $107,315	B
45	One easement for a power line is an example of this. (A) easement in gross. (B) easement by prescription. (C) appurtenant easement. (D) easement by necessity.	A
46	The ad valorem methodology is a method of determining the monetary worth of something. (A) appraise property. (B) determine market value (C) determine a listing price. D) assess property.	D

47	An acknowledgement is a statement made by one of the contractual parties that the other party has received the acknowledgement. (A) is authorized to enter into the contract. (B) is of sound mind. (C) entered into the contract freely. (D) is the party named in the contract.	C
48	James and Marie Pappas are selling Mr. James' home, which has three bedrooms, two and a half bathrooms, and is 2,550 square feet in size. A home in the same area has just sold for $375,600, according to public records. The house is 2,500 square feet in size and has four bedrooms and two bathrooms in total. What is the market value of Mr. James' home if the bedrooms are worth $15,000 and the bathrooms are worth $7,500? (A) $356,838 (B) $362,974 (C) $387,963 (D) $394,362	A
49	While trying to sell a house, the realtor will utilize an exclusive agency listing to do so. (A) receives a commission no matter who sells the property. (B) receives a commission only if he or she sells the property. (C) has to be paid a commission if the seller sells the property without any help. (D) receives a reduced commission if the seller sells the property himself or herself.	B
50	All of the elements of a conforming mortgage are included in one package: EXCEPT FOR THE FACTORY (A) meets the criteria for sale to Fannie Mae and Freddie Mac. (B) is a conventional mortgage. (C) is a fixed rate mortgage. (D) is a jumbo mortgage.	D

Practice Test 6

Question Number	Question	Answer
1	Which of the following is NOT one of the factors that impact the value of a home under the control of the federal government? (A) Property taxes (B) Zoning (C) Interest rates (D) Building codes	C
2	John Hall left his whole inheritance, including his real estate, to his crippled son, who is now the only beneficiary of his will. Assuming the son's daughter survives him, his inheritance (which includes the real estate) will be passed to her when he dies. A "daughter" is the term used to refer to the child. (A) revector. (B) sublessee. (C) remainderman. (D) subordinate inheritor.	C
3	A real estate broker receives a 7 percent commission on the first $150,000 of a home's sale price and a 3 percent commission on each additional dollar beyond $150,000. When a home offered for $240,000 sells for $220,000, what is the commission loss to the real estate agent? (A) $2,700 (B) $10,500 (C) $1,116 (D) $1,584	D
4	It was explained to Shirley Jordan that she possessed equitable title to her recently bought property, but that the bank had legal title. The state where she lives must be one that bases its mortgage laws on the Constitution. (A) lien theory. (B) title abstract theory. (C) title theory. (D) transitional theory.	C
5	Three points have been paid on the mortgage of Anita Oshodi by her decision. How much is she paying in points if her mortgage is for $354,000? (A) $106.20 (B) $1,062 (C) $10,620 (D) $106,200	C

6	Mortgagees attempt to close on their properties as soon as possible in order to limit the amount of interest that accrues before the first monthly mortgage payment. (A) the first day of the month. (B) the fifteenth of the month. (C) the last day of the month. (D) When a closing occurs doesn't affect the amount of interest accrued.	C
7	In a case of housing discrimination, an administrative law court may impose all of the following sanctions WITH THE EXCEPTION OF (A) payment of a fine to the federal government. (B) payment of damages, which include humiliation, pain, and suffering, to the complainant. (C) injunctive or other forms of relief such as making the property available to the complainant. (D) closing the building.	D
8	In a contract for deed, the buyer is referred to as a (A) vendor. (B) vendee. (C) lessor. (D) lessee	B
9	The service station on Mulberry Street is worth $52,000, according to its appraiser. Businesses in the municipality pay a 6.5 mills rate on their profits. The rate will rise to 8.2 mills per cent the following year. What is the amount of the tax disparity that the station will be required to bear? (A) $426.40 (B) $88.40 (C) $126.40 (D) $27.40	B
10	Which of the following is accomplished by an alienation provision in a mortgage? (A) States the type of foreclosure that can be used by the lender to take posession of the property if the mortgage defaults (B) Provides for how the ownership will be divided in a non community property state should the owner's divorce (C) States the mortgagee will have full title to the property once the mortgage is paid in full (D) Requires that a buyer assuming the mortgage on the property from the current buyer be approved by the lender	D
11	The Oliver's will be the sellers in an escrow closing. They must give which of the following to the escrow agent before the closure may take place before the closing? (A) Certified check to pay off their mortgage (B) Homeowner's insurance policy	C

	(C) Executed deed to their property (D) Proof of title insurance	
12	In order to supplement his income while working for a computer firm and travelling overseas for months at a time, Al Janssen sublets his flat. His previous renter has refused to vacate the premises at the conclusion of the sublet, resulting in a/an eviction. (A) periodic tenancy. (B) estate at sufferance. (C) estate at will. (D) tenancy by possession.	B
13	It costs $234.60 to pay the first month's interest on a one-year loan for $34,000 at an interest rate of 8.2 percent. What is the amount of interest paid in the second month if the monthly installments are $2,962.01, including interest? (A) $234.60 (B) $215.78 (C) $220.98 (D) $235.90	B
14	At the time of a closure, which of the following items is normally the first to be paid off? (A) Property tax lien dated September 15, 2009 (B) Materialman's lien dated May 12, 2010 (C) IRS income tax lien dated January 19, 2010 (D) Lien for nonpayment of water and sewer utilities dated August 21, 2009	C
15	Ebony Baxter has signed a two-year lease on an apartment maintained by Realty Inc. in the heart of downtown Los Angeles. The rent will rise by 2 percent at the conclusion of the first year under the contract. What form of lease has she agreed to be bound by? (A) Percentage lease (B) Step lease (C) Graduated lease (D) Net lease	C
16	Who is it that is interested in Ebony's residence in the above example? (A) Leased fee interest (B) Leasehold estate (C) Lessor interest (D) None	B
17	On May 30, a farmhouse went under the hammer for $687,432. If the real estate taxes of $6,038.60 are not paid in full for one year on September 15, who is liable and how much is owed to whom? (A) $4,277.31 to the seller (B) $3,774.21 to the seller (C) $3,774.21 to the buyer (D) $4,277.31 to the buyer	D

18	Jasper is considering whether she should use her cash to purchase an apartment or to make an investment in an online jeweler firm. By owning the condominium, she foregoes the possibility to benefit from a company, but the condo is a solid investment. What economic theory is it that has her in such a bind? (A) Contribution (B) Increasing returns (C) Supply and demand (D) Opportunity cost	D
19	Which of the following factors is NOT taken into consideration when valuing unimproved land? (A) Location (B) Financing (C) Any restrictions on property rights (D) Siting	D
20	The property of a local furniture shop was sold after 12 years of appreciation at an average rate of 8 percent each year. It was initially purchased for a sum of $653,800. What was the most recent selling price? (A) $627,648 (B) $1,281,448 (C) $607,104 (D) $1,265,439	B
21	As a result, Win Farrell contacts his next-door neighbor, Jack Straw, a real estate agent, for help in selling his house. Before bringing some prospective buyers through the door, Jack offers Win some staging suggestions. One of the couples makes a proposal, which Jack offers to Win, who accepts it without hesitation. Win is then accompanied by Jack all the way to the finale. What kind of agency does Jack have as a result of his partnership with Win? (A) Agency by ratification (B) Agency by estoppels (C) Express agency (D) Agency coupled with an interest	A
22	Jerry March, who lives next door to Jack, approaches him and expresses his concern that Jack would show the home to any of "those people." Jack's best answer should be that he is sorry but (A) will show the house to anyone who will fit into the neighborhood. (B) doesn't know what Jerry means. (C) will show the property to anyone who has adequate finances to buy the house. (D) has to show the house to anyone who wants to buy a house.	C
23	If, like in the preceding example, Jack exclusively showed the home to young white married couples, he would be engaging in practice.	C

	(A) redlining. (B) discrimination based on familial status. (C) steering. (D) bundling.	

24	In what proportion of an acreage does a township take up? (A) 640 (B) 4,840 (C) 5,280 (D) 43,560	A
25	Two adjacent farms are being offered for sale in order to be developed. One such parcel, which covered 173 acres, was just sold for $759,000. What is the worth of the other property if it is 143 acres? (A) $642,987 (B) $918,230 (C) $627,381 (D) $759,000	C
26	WITH THE EXCEPTION of the following, everything is documented after a close. (A) the mortgage. (B) liens. (C) inspection reports. (D) easements.	C
27	In terms of disclosing significant information that has an impact on the value or usage of a property, a realtor w. (A) doesn't have to disclose anything more than is on the seller's disclosure form. (B) has to disclose anything that he or she knows is of a material nature regardless of what is on the form. (C) has a fiduciary duty to the seller to protect the seller's best interest and so must abide by what the seller discloses. (D) has no responsibility; it is the seller's responsibility only.	B
28	When a listing agreement is reached, it results in the termination of the arrangement. (A) the term of the agreement has expired and the agent has worked conscientiously to bring buyers to the property. (B) an agent brings an offer from a ready, willing, and able buyer to a seller who accepts the offer. (C) the seller terminates the agency because of a perceived lack of interest in the listing by the realtor. (D) the seller and the broker agree to end the agreement because of a lack of concurrence on what the broker should be doing.	B
29	A shared tenancy requires the possession of unities of (A) time, title, interest, and control. (B) title, possession, interest, and consideration.	C

	(C) time, interest, title, and possession. (D) title, control, survivorship, and possession.	

30	What is the estimated cost of the concrete required to pave the Lewis' driveway, which is 80 feet long, 14 feet wide, and 6 inches deep? The concrete is $105 per cubic yard and is produced in-house. (A) $2,178.75 (B) $2,205 (C) $2,100 (D) $26,133.33	A
31	Which of the following kinds of ownership does not have a right to concurrent ownership, and why? (A) Tenancy in severalty (B) Tenancy by the entirety (C) Community property (D) Joint tenancy	A
32	A real estate broker that works in a dual agency is known as a dual agent... (A) acts solely as an intermediary between seller and buyer. (B) shares listings with other brokers. (C) represents both the seller and the buyer in a transaction. (D) sells real estate as well as acts as a property manager for some clients.	C
33	An aged elevator would be taken into consideration during an evaluation as a/an asset. (A) curable physical deterioration (B) curable economic obsolescence. (C) incurable functional obsolescence. (D) curable functional obsolescence.	A
34	A typical listing agreement will contain all of the items listed below WITH THE EXCEPTION OF (A) zoning. (B) property taxes. (C) type of agency created by the listing agreement. (D) closing date.	D
35	An assignment of a lease is a legal document. (A) partial transfer of rights between landlord and lessee. (B) partial transfer of rights from sub- lessor to sublease. (C) total transfer of rights from lessee to a third party. (D) total transfer of rights from sublease to sub lessee.	C
36	Broker Chris Phillips has a contract to sell a parcel of land on Oak Lane, which is located in the neighborhood. He will earn 3 percent of the first $25,000 and 7.5 percent of every dollar beyond that amount in subsequent years. If his commission is $1,800, what was the selling price of the property? (A) $14,000 (B) $39,000	B

	(C) $25,000	
	(D) $1,050	

37	Select the statement that best represents subprime mortgages out of the following options. (A) Subprime mortgages originate in the subprime mortgage market. (B) Subprime mortgages are taken out by borrowers with good credit ratings. (C) Subprime mortgages are more likely to go to foreclosure than other types of mortgages. (D) Subprime mortgages are fixed-rate mortgages only.	C
38	The distinction between earnest money and a down payment is that the buyer's money is held in trust for the seller. (A) agent requires earnest money with the listing, and the seller requires a down payment with the sales contract. (B) lender requires a down payment, and the seller requires earnest money. (C) lender requires earnest money, and the seller requires a down payment. (D) lender requires earnest money, and the seller's lender requires a down payment. practice	B
39	Which of the following is regarded to be fraudulent behavior on the part of a real estate agent? (A) Failure to display the Fair Housing poster (B) Failure to submit all offers to the seller (C) Acting as if one is employed by a seller or buyer when one is not (D) Failure to maintain contact with one's principal between offer delivery and acceptance and the closing	C
40	Which of the following best characterizes the allocation of market resources? (A) Stan Bailey and Ed James of South Side Realty decide to carve up the South Side district between them looking for properties to list. (B) Stan Bailey of South Side Realty and Bob Wood of First-Rate Realty meet over lunch to discuss how they might combine their money to advertise listings on the South Side. (C) Stan Bailey of South Side Realty and Bob Wood of First-Rate Realty meet on January 2 to decide what commission rate their agencies will charge for the coming year. (D) Stan Bailey of South Side Realty and Bob Wood of First-Rate Realty meet on January 2 and decide which agency will sell duplexes and which will sell stand-alone homes in the district.	D
41	Al Simone will pay $5,000 in interest over the course of a two-year loan for $75,000 in total. What is the interest rate at which he is being penalized for this? (A) 0.278%	C

	(B) 6 2/3 % 1	
	(C) 3 /3 % 1	
	(D) 4/ 2 %	

42	It is the brother of John Girardi who is pressuring him to sell his vacation house in a neighboring state. Joe, who has a broker's license in his home state, (A) must decline unless he gets a license in the adjoining state. (B) must ask a broker friend to sign him on as an independent contractor for that one sale. (C) can sell the property on his own without any special arrangements. (D) can get a temporary permit from the adjoining state's real estate com- mission for this one sale.	A
43	A real estate brokerage owner who is also a franchisee of a major real estate business qualifies for all of the franchisee advantages listed below. EXCEPT (A) national branding of his or her local office. (B) a bonus if the office meets its sales goals. (C) access to technology tools such as Internet marketing. (D) attendance at sales training workshops.	B
44	It was recently determined that Trevor's home was worth $357,840, according to a new appraisal. Assuming the house's assessment rate is 63%, and the school district tax rate is 6.5 mills, as well as the county tax rate of 3.25 mills, what is the house's true worth? (A) $348,894 (B) $553,008 (C) $568,000 (D) $687,439	C
45	According to Regulation Z, which of the following loans is exempt? (A) Commercial mortgages (B) VA-guaranteed mortgages (C) Mortgages on owner-occupied premises of 4 or fewer units (D) FHA-insured mortgages	A
46	It is necessary to provide the borrower with a Mortgage Loan Disclosure Statement. (A) within 48 hours of applying for the mortgage. (B) within 3 days of applying for the mortgage. (C) within 10 business days of applying for the mortgage. (D) the day before the closing.	B
47	Freddie Mac and Fannie Mae need a loan's loan-to-value ratio to be less than 50% in order for the loan to be considered acceptable. (A) 80/20. (B) less than 80 percent. (C) less than or equal to 80 percent. (D) more than 80 percent.	C

48	New, the value of your vacation property was $1,357,990. What would be the depreciation per year if you were to depreciate it over a period of 25 years using straight-line depreciation? (A) $45,319.60 (B) $54,319.60 (C) $108.639.20 (D) $81,639.20	B
49	Chet Murray is evaluating a school property on behalf of a developer who intends to convert it into condominiums. Which methodology would Chet most likely utilize as the primary means of determining the value of the property? (A) Cost approach (B) Sales comparison approach (C) Use value approach (D) Income approach	D
50	A 14-unit apartment complex with rents averaging $1,250 per month has just been sold. What was the cost of the building if the buyer was instructed to anticipate a 9.5 percent return on his investment? (A) $2,210,526 (B) $221,052 (C) $210,000 (D) $2,100,000	A

Practice Test 7

Question Number	Question	Answer
1	With a 7% fee, the neighborhood Mini Mart sold for $1,280,000, including the commission. If the seller's broker earned $51,072, what was the percentage of the commission? (A) 0.57 (B) 0.67 (C) 0.77 (D) 0.87	A
2	With a 7% fee, the neighborhood Mini Mart sold for $1,280,000, including the commission. If the seller's broker earned $51,072, what was the percentage of the commission? (A) 0.57 (B) 0.67 (C) 0.77 (D) 0.87	B
3	A loan that amortizes is one in which the principal and interest are paid off over time. (A) the amount of principal that is paid down increases over time, while the amount of the interest paid stays the same. (B) the amount of principal that is paid down decreases over time, while the amount of the interest that is paid increases. (C) the amount of principal that is paid down increases over time, while the amount of interest that is paid decreases. (D) the amounts of both principal and interest remain the same for the term of the loan.	A
4	Regulation Z is strictly adhered to. (A) fair housing laws. (B) hazardous materials laws . (C) consumer credit laws. (D) the mortgage industry.	D
5	The rights to use and enjoy one's property are included in the package of rights that come with real estate ownership. (A) sell interests in the property, lease the property, use the property. (B) bequeath the property, lease the property, depreciate the property. (C) sell interests in the property, apple- cite the property, use the property. (D) donate the property, depreciate the property, do nothing with the property.	C

6	Earnest money is a sum of money paid as a deposit. (A) another name for a down payment. (B) used for recording and transfer fees. (C) used to pay the seller's broker if the buyer defaults. (D) the amount requested by the seller to bind the buyer to the sales contract.	C
7	It is referred to as a second mortgage if it is paid after another mortgage in the event of a default by the mortgagor. (A) minor mortgage. (B) lower-grade mortgage. (C) subprime mortgage. (D) junior mortgage.	A
8	The lender will need all of the pre-paid items listed below at closing, with the exception of the following: (A) mortgage insurance premiums. (B) hazard insurance premiums. (C) appraisal fee. (D) property taxes.	D
9	The property owned by Lewis James was appraised at $2,204,000 dollars. Prior to this, the tax rate per $100 of income was $4.50. Following the passage of a new school finance law, the new cost is $6.50 every $100 of spending. The difference between his monthly tax bill and the one that came before it is unclear. (A) $3,673.33 (B) $44,080 (C) $9,918 (D) $14,326	D
10	A benefit of a VA-guaranteed mortgage is that it is less expensive. (A) no private mortgage insurance is required regardless of the amount of the down payment. (B) the down payment can be as low as 3 percent. (C) that it can be used to buy a rental property as well as a primary residence . (D) that credit rating is not considered by the lender in determining eligibility for a mortgage. practice	C
11	This is a house that the Oliver's are purchasing in a community that has an assessment ratio of 52 percent. This implies that they will compensate you. (A) a tax rate of 52 percent. (B) a tax rate of $0.52. (C) taxes on 52 percent of the value of their home. (D) taxes on 48 percent of the value of their home.	A

12	All of the following conditions must be met in order for a real estate transaction to be considered an arm's length deal EXCEPT (A) all parties are ready, willing, and able to complete the transaction. (B) no pressure has been exerted on any parties. (C) everyone has the same set of facts about the transaction. (D) the transaction is an "as is" transaction.	A
13	When doing an environmental assessment, which of the following stages estimates the cost of remediating a site? (A) Phase I (B) Phase II (C) Phase III (D) Phase IV	C
14	A buyer should request which of the following from the lender in order to ensure that the terms of the mortgage at the time of closing are the same as those that the borrower believed them to be? (A) Certificate of Torrens (B) Certificate of estoppels (C) Certificate of title (D) Abstract of title	D
15	During Tamika Johnson's 18-year ownership period, her property has depreciated at a rate of 3 percent each year. What is the current market worth of the property if she purchased it for $132,000? (A) $60,720 (B) $71,280 (C) $83,265 (D) $95,737	C
16	In the process of acquiring their first home, Jake and Marita Morales have come across a great deal of information. Due to the fact that they do not dwell in a state that recognizes common property or tenancy by the whole, they will most likely be the sole owners of their property. (A) joint tenancy. (B) tenancy in common. (C) tenancy in severalty. (D) tenancy at will.	B
17	The city purchases a block of condemned dwellings, demolishes them, and turns the area into a park. The city needed the purchase of land in order to construct the park. (A) nonconforming use zoning. (B) density zoning. (C) spot zoning. (D) open space zoning.	A

18	The highest penalties a realtor may get if he or she is found guilty of two or more breaches of the Fair Housing Act within seven years is $10,000. (A) $11,000. (B) $22,000. (C) $55,000 . (D) $100,000.	A
19	A multi-family building is purchased as a long-term investment by Sam Knowles, John Hudson, and Brian Morgan Tenancy in common (also known as joint tenancy) (A) each had to put in the same amount of money. (B) each may sell his interest whenever he wishes. (C) none of them can take out a mortgage on his interest without the consent of the others. (D) should one of them die, the others will inherit his third.	C
20	Which of the following legislation protects property owners from having their properties taken away to settle debts other than mortgage debts in certain states? (A) Homestead property exemption (B) Nonprofit property exemption (C) Nonprofit property tax exemption (D) Fee simple ownership	C
21	The following terms and conditions apply to the exclusive right to sell listing: EXCEPT (A) ensuring that the seller's broker will be paid the commission regardless of who finds the buyer. (B) giving the seller's broker the sole right to market the property. (C) allowing the seller to sell his or her own property. (D) not allowing the property to be listed on an MLS.	B
22	The renting of a local office building generates a profit of $1,050 per month on average. What is the worth of the property if the investment yields a 7 percent return? (A) $11,666 (B) $180,000 (C) $116,666 (D) $18,000	A
23	A judgement lien is a legal claim. (A) general lien. (B) specific lien. (C) voluntary lien. (D) minor lien.	D
24	When it comes to the secondary mortgage market, which of the following assertions is correct? (A) The secondary mortgage market provides mortgages to mortgagors. (B) The secondary mortgage market requires that mortgages have PMI.	B

	(C) Investors buy mortgage-backed securities on the secondary mortgage market. (D) Fannie Mae insures mortgages that are sold on the secondary mortgage market.	
25	Recent acquisition by the Barbers of a riverfront property with 110 feet of river frontage. When you have a property that is half an acre in size, how deep is the property? (A) 404' (B) 198' (C) 396' (D) 202	A
26	The Rex family purchased their house for $175,000 ten years ago, putting down 10% of the purchase price and taking out a $157,500 mortgage. The outstanding main balance is at $98,900. When it comes to their house, how much equity do the Rex's have overall? (A) $17,500 (B) $58,600 (C) $76,100 (D) $116,400 practice	C
27	Price fixing is prohibited. (A) what an agent does in deciding at what price to list a property. (B) what the appraiser does in adjusting the value of comps to the subject property. (C) the collusion between two or more realtors in an area to set the sales commission rate. (D) the adjustment that a seller and agent do when they reduce the sale price of a property because it isn't moving.	B
28	The following are the primary components of a typical mortgage payment: (A) principal, interest, property taxes. (B) principal, interest, private mortgage insurance, property taxes. (C) principal, interest, homeowner's insurance, property tax. (D) principal, interest, points, property taxes.	C
29	The town has chosen to construct a pedestrian walkway on both sides of Cherry Valley Road. What kind of easement will be generated as a consequence of this decision? (A) Appurtenant easement (B) Easement in gross (C) Easement by prescription (D) Easement by necessity	C
30	Which of the following would be protected under the notion of familiar status if you were to rent a house? (A) Elderly parent moving in with daughter and family (B) Roommates who are cousins (C) Pregnant single woman (D) Unmarried couple	C

31	He is looking to sell his seven-bedroom house on Elm Street, which he has owned for more than 20 years. A six-bedroom property in the region just sold for $75,000, according to the local real estate market. What is the monetary value of Horace's home? (A) $62,500 (B) $75,000 (C) $81,500 (D) $87,500	B
32	The Allied family has accepted an offer on their house and is now awaiting the signature of the purchase agreement with the seller. Which of the following statements is the most accurate depiction of the current state of affairs? (A) The Allied' agent may not continue to show the property. (B) The Allied may not entertain any offers that other agents bring to them. (C) Other agents must stop showing the property. (D) The Allied may accept back-up offers.	C
33	For the purpose of locating apartment complexes for Peter James to acquire, providing information on the properties, and negotiating on his behalf, Martinson Realty has been engaged by Peter James. Martinson Realty is acting in the role of an agent or representatives. (A) universal agent. (B) agent by estoppel. (C) special agent. (D) general agent.	D
34	Peter James is contemplating acquiring the apartment complex owned by the Johnson Company as a long-term investment. Identify which of the following will be most helpful in assessing how long the building will continue to provide value to the property? (A) Economic life (B) Physical life (C) Effective age (D) Actual age	D
35	All of the following are covered by federal rules governing municipal solid waste landfills, with the exception of (A) restrictions on locations of landfills. (B) disposal of radioactive wastes. (C) monitoring of groundwater. (D) requirements related to the closure of landfills.	C
36	Sue Lewis of Rana Resort Realty has exclusive marketing rights to the Woodlands development. On the first $100,000 in sales, she receives a 6 percent fee, and on every dollar sold after that, she receives a 7 percent commission. What was her total commission check when she sold three homes in March, with prices ranging from $89,000 to $97,000 and $82,000? (A) $6,000	A

	(B) $17,420 (C) $17,760 (D) $22,780	
37	In order to calculate square footage, (A) multiply length times width. (B) add length and width and multiply by 2. (C) add length and width. (D) multiple length times width and divide by the cost per square foot.	B
38	Title XI of the federal Financial Institutions Reform, Recovery, and Enforcement Act (FIRREA) governs the regulation of financial institutions. (A) real estate licensing (B) real estate appraising. (C) the secondary mortgage markets. (D) the primary mortgage markets.	C
39	The civil penalty that the Department of Housing and Urban Development (HUD) may impose for fraud in interstate land transactions is a $10,000 fine. (A) maximum of $1,000 in any one year. (B) maximum of $10,000 in any one year. (C) maximum of $1 million in any one year. (D) $1 million lifetime maximum.	A
40	The Mays brothers are putting together a subdivision of property and have obtained a contract for deed on the Lewis farm. The Mays will be able to take advantage of this circumstance. (A) take title immediately while paying off the purchase price in installments. (B) borrow the purchase price from a financial institution over a longer period of time. (C) take title after a certain number of monthly payments have been made . (D) negotiate for a wraparound mortgage with a bank.	B
41	Three-thirds of a triangular lot with a frontage of 335' and a depth of 172' has a frontage of 335' and a depth of 172'. What is the commission rate if the commission rate is 6 percent and the land sells for $2.55 per square foot when the commission rate is 6 percent? (A) $4,407.93 (B) $440.79 (C) $44,079.3 (D) $440,793	C

42	The Floyds are in the process of purchasing their first home. They will need to borrow $200,000 and put down a 20 percent down payment on the house. They are looking for a 30-year fixed-rate mortgage with an interest rate of 5.1 percent. It will cost them $2,340 per month in housing payments, which will cover the loan's principal, interest, taxes, and homeowner's insurance. If they have a total income of $80,090, what percentage of their combined monthly salary will be spent on household expenses? (A) 2.85 percent (B) 28.5 percent (C) 3.5 percent (D) 35 percent	C
43	Would the Floyds be eligible for a $200,000 loan based on the widely recognized mortgage criteria that the sum of monthly mortgage, tax, and any other housing debt payments cannot exceed "X" percent of gross monthly income? Would the Floyds qualify for a $200,000 loan based on the widely recognized mortgage criteria that the sum of monthly mortgage, tax, and any other housing debt payments cannot exceed "X" percent of gross monthly income (A) Yes, because the percentage of the sum of the payments less than the guidelines. (B) Yes, because the percentage of the sum of the payments is just equal to the guidelines. (C) No, because their housing payments are already at the limit without including the monthly no housing payments. (D) Can't answer the question because there is no information on the Floyds' other debt payments.	A
44	To be lawful, a deed must have all of the elements listed below WITHOUT the exception of (A) habendum clause (B) defeasance clause. (C) granting clause. (D) consideration.	D
45	Which of the following should be recorded as a payment to the seller on a broker's reconciliation worksheet? (A) Real estate commission (B) Mortgage recording fee (C) Amount of the balance on the purchase price (D) Pest inspection fee	C
46	There are various different forms of insurance for a rental building. In order to effectively manage a property, which of the following is recommended? (A) Fire and hazard insurance (B) Errors and omissions insurance (C) Casualty insurance (D) Rent loss insurance	B

47	Typically, rents are predetermined. (A) after an analysis of the building by a certified appraiser. (B) somewhat arbitrarily. (C) based on the expenses of the building. (D) based on market rents and vacancy rates.	D
48	Sally is a salesperson that works for Broker Bob. Despite Bob's knowledge, Sally has shown an especially hostile attitude toward Vietnamese consumers. Will Broker Bob be held liable if she is charged with a fair housing violation if she is charged with one? (A) Yes (B) No (C) Only if she is an employee (D) Only if Bob had known	A
49	When a property manager does a risk assessment on a facility, he or she may propose all except which of the following? (A) Retain risk (B) Transfer risk (C) Avoid risk (D) Contain risk	D
50	During their meeting, Broker A and Broker B discuss a listing that both of them are currently working on. They talk about the commission they will each get. Which of the following statements is correct? (A) They have violated antitrust laws on price fixing. (B) They have violated local real estate board practice if the fee they are discussing is beyond the standard fee schedule. (C) They really can't discuss anything because the state real estate commission sets fees. (D) No violation of the law has occurred.	D

CONCLUSION

You should be proud of yourself for completing the book. A real estate license takes investment of both time and money, but it may lead to a rewarding career in the real estate industry with possibilities for promotion if you work hard and persevere.

In order to operate as a real estate salesperson or provisional broker, you will need to be employed by and under the supervision of a licensed broker. You may finally decide to pursue a broker or broker-in-charge license in order to have greater flexibility and opportunities in the working world.

As a real estate professional, you may wish to consider real estate designations and certifications, such as those in mortgage lending, appraisals, residential property management, commercial property management and property management, to further your career and increase your marketability.

Good Luck!

SPECIAL BONUS

Dear user, I would appreciate it if you would spend a minute of your time and post a **short review on AMAZON** to let other users know about this experience and what you liked most about the book. Also, as of recently I decided to do a giveaway to all our readers. Yes, I want to give you **4 gifts.**

1. To help you with your study, **the audiobook will be free for you**. It will help you to go over the information by listening to it and imprinting the concepts in your mind. You will surely enjoy the interactive tests: you will have time to reflect and learn dynamically.

2. You will also receive a **pdf with practical tips** that we hope will help you focus and pass your exam with flying colors.

3. **FLASHCARDS TO USE FOR FREE online or offline!** You can track your progress and conveniently and interactively memorize the most important terms and concepts! Download to your device: _Anki APP or AnkiDroid, or enter the web page and register free of charge._ Then import the files we have given you as a gift and use the flashcards whenever and wherever you want to study and track your progress.

4. **750 Q&As** to continue to prepare fruitfully for the exam and pass it stress-free

Below you will find a QR CODE that will give you direct access to these bonuses _without having to subscribe to any mailing list or leave your data._
We hope you enjoy it.
To communicate with us directly, please write to us at
readers.help.info@gmail.com
A friendly greeting, we wish you the best.

Made in United States
North Haven, CT
26 September 2023

41998021R10089